A LAWYER'S GUIDE TO

CREATING A

LIFE

NOT JUST A LIVING

Ordinary Lawyers Doing Extraordinary Things

Paula Black

BlackBox
PUBLISHING & DISTRIBUTION

Published by Black Box Publishing

For more information, contact: info@paulablack.com

Printed: September 2018

ISBN: 978-0-9768285-6-3 (paperback)

ISBN: 978-0-9768285-7-0 (e-book)

Cover design by: Layne Mitchell, Layne Creative Services

Interior design by: Patrizia Sceppa, Inc.

Printed in the United States of America

I dedicate this book, a labor of love, to my mother, Helen Lucero, who instilled in me a good work ethic and a belief that I can do anything I set my mind to. And in her eighties, Mom reminds me that I'll never be too old to follow my passion.

I have lived in Miami for over thirty years, and it is said you can never go home again. Not so. In 2012, I made the decision to spend more time with my mother. It was in the middle of the recession, and figuring out a way seemed insurmountable. But where there's a will, there's a way.

And a wonderful thing happened. I landed on the solution: open a Denver office to do what I do—help lawyers with business and professional development. It has proven to be the best decision I have ever made. The time I'm spending with my mother and family is priceless. And being on the board of the Denver based non-profit *Law School...Yes We Can* has been inspiring.

Thank you to everyone who has welcomed me home.

Paula Black

CONTENTS

Introduction
To Begin With

Welcome! Thank you for purchasing this book. A portion of the proceeds will go to *Law School...Yes We Can*, a nonprofit pipeline-mentoring program dedicated to advancing diversity and inclusion in the legal profession. And I thank you.

Let me tell you how this book came about. I have been speaking to and coaching lawyers for many, many years, and in doing so, I've observed the many challenges, obstacles, and myths lawyers face as they pursue advancement in their careers, grow their practices, and try to fit it all into their lives. These are the ten bedrock principles that I discovered help lawyers advance in the profession without sacrificing their personal lives.

- Embrace change. Most lawyers resist change. Life isn't a straight line—it zigzags from one point to another. Be ready to identify opportunities that could be life-altering, and open to pursuing them.

- Find your passion, your north star. When you know what fuels you and focus on it, more of it will come your way.

- Make a commitment! It's the essential ingredient that will move mountains. Without commitment there is little progress, only lateral movement that is no better than stagnation.

- Examine your assumptions. Are you pre-programmed with what you should do, with no room for what you want to do? Rewrite your program.

- Don't let fear hold you back. Fear will always be there, that's a given. It's what we do in the face of it. Achieve the success you define for yourself, in spite of the fear.

- You can do it your way. Break the rules. Challenge the status quo. You just may find the perfect path for your life.

- Find a niche. Something that will set you apart from the six million other lawyers on this planet.

- Tailor your work to fit in harmony with your life. And don't waste one minute feeling inadequate. No one gets to define your work-life balance but you.

- Prepare for your third act. Create it on your own terms through the lens of your passion, your calling, and your heart.

- Build relationships that matter. Relationships that are genuine and authentic lead you down the path to professional and personal fulfillment.

To illustrate these principles I have interviewed twenty-two lawyers and four experts. They come from the public defender's office and the city attorney's office, from solo practices and big national firms, from corporate settings and government, from academia and the bench. They are Judge Christine Arguello, Dr. Joseph Ramos, Maia Aron, Denver Doxilly, Laura Reich, Judge Roberto Ramirez, Candice Duff, Miko Brown, Michelle Otero Valdes, Karen Lapekas, Dr. Elyse Hurtado, Joshua Hertz, Judge Alex Bokor, Daniel Benavides, Michelle Estlund, Antonio Gallegos, Marc Cerniglia, Daniel Decker, Suzanne Ferguson, Mark Yonkman, Terry Vento, Lorenzo Trujillo, John Kozyak, Cathy Pareto, Clarissa Rodriguez, and Marlon Hill.

I thank them for sharing their challenges, insights and solutions. You will read about what they overcame to have a sense of fulfillment, what they discovered about themselves, and how they achieved their equilibrium. And I guarantee their words will move and inspire you.

They created a life, not just a living. When you apply the principles in this book, you can do the same. And to help you get started on your own path I provide you with a complimentary assessment tool at the end of this book. It will help you take a look at your own situation and provide you with a roadmap to creating a life.

Chapter One

Life Isn't a Straight Line

Life isn't usually a straight line—lock step advancement.

It zigzags from one point to another. It doesn't follow neat and orderly tracks. So I ask you, are you in the driver's seat, or are you just along for the ride? Are you reading the signs, or is your head down, absorbed in your own little world as it is today?

When you're out of your comfort zone, do you look for a new route, or do you stay put?

Let me ask you, do things seem to be going wrong lately? Maybe it's the universe telling you something. Maybe you shouldn't be there. Maybe you shouldn't be where you are. Maybe there's something better waiting for you.

There are signs all around us. They are trying to tell us to turn left or right, move forward or make a bold move.

As one grows, life experiences offer opportunities and new mountains to climb. Should we take them? Or should we resign ourselves to the decisions that were made so many years ago?

I say take them! Grab the brass ring and sign up for the challenges to conquer new heights. You never know where it may lead.

That's exactly what these two lawyers did—Judge Christine Arguello and Dr. Joseph Ramos.

Judge Christine Arguello was partner in two major firms, a tenured full professor, the chief deputy attorney general of the state of Colorado, in-house counsel, and the first Hispanic United States district court judge for the District of Colorado. That, my friends, is not a straight line.

Judge Arguello always signed up for the challenge to conquer new heights and she thrives on change.

Judge Christine Arguello
U.S. District Court Judge,
District of Colorado

"*Unfortunately, many people stay in situations in which they are unhappy and unfulfilled merely because they are afraid of change. I have never been afraid of change.*"

Black: Judge, if you had to describe your path to success, what would that be?

Arguello: A few years back, my law clerks and I were sitting around the conference table in my chambers eating lunch, and as I usually do, I like to delve into their personae. So I asked them, "How is it that you find yourself sitting at this table with a federal judge? If you had to describe your path to professional success as a lawyer in just a few words, what would those words be?"

They responded with the usual list of success criteria: high GPA, good LSAT score, interest in the law. Then they asked me the same question, "How is it that you find yourself sitting at this table as a federal judge?"

I have thought about this question for many years, because I give a lot of inspirational speeches to students and others in the community. So they were surprised when I immediately responded, "Big dreams, hard work, and a lot of serendipity."

Now, the first two, big dreams and hard work—go hand in hand, and they understood that. But they were a little perplexed about the third element, serendipity.

Black: How does serendipity play into the equation?

Arguello: As I look back on my life, there is no other way to put it. Serendipity, which is fortunate happenstance, played a significant role in defining the path my life would take. Indeed, the only reason I even became a lawyer was because at age thirteen, I happened to pick up a magazine that contained an article on lawyers and law schools. And when I read that article, it was like lightning struck me. Until that day, it had never even occurred to me that I could be a lawyer.

Now, that is hardly surprising, considering my background. Neither of my parents had graduated from high school, and I didn't know any lawyers, or other professionals for that matter, other than my teachers and my dentist. In fact, all I knew about lawyers was what I had seen on television: they liked to argue. So did I! And I usually won my arguments. So, as simply as that, I decided I could make a pretty good lawyer.

Now, the article went on to mention that Harvard Law School was the best law school in the country. And isn't that what I wanted for myself? I wanted the best. So one naive thought led to another, and at age thirteen, I found myself with a mission. I was going to be a lawyer, and I was going to attend Harvard Law School. Oh, what big dreams for a small-town seventh grader who did not know anything about Harvard, not even where it was located.

Black: Did serendipity show up again?

Arguello: Throughout my life, serendipity interwove itself. I have worked hard for everything I have ever achieved, but to have the career I have had, hard work alone is often not enough. I was able to succeed as a lawyer in both private and public settings, as a private practitioner, an academic, chief deputy attorney general, in-house counsel for my undergrad alma mater, the University of Colorado at Boulder, and now as a federal judge, because I have the guidance, advice, and support of incredible mentors. By choice, I've held a lot of very different legal jobs. But I never left a job on a low note. I always accomplished my goal, which was the means by which I measured my success: Make partner in a law firm. Become a tenured professor. Efficiently manage the court docket.

Black: When did you have your first "Aha!" moment?

Arguello: The first "aha" moment in my professional life came when I was a law student who naively thought that because of my Harvard Law degree, law firms would be rushing with open arms to welcome me to join the litigation sections of their firms. However, I quickly came to understand that I did not fit the stereotype of a successful trial lawyer that the Colorado law firms envisioned. In other words, I was not a male.

Remember, this was in the late 1970s, and there were very few women trial attorneys in Colorado and there were no Latina trial attorneys. Add to that that I looked very young for my age and was a petite five foot two inches tall and weighed about ninety pounds soaking wet. The recruiters kept trying to talk me into becoming a transactional lawyer. So this was my first "aha" moment. If I wanted to be a trial attorney, which was my goal, then I had to take charge of my own life. And if that meant not going back home to Colorado, so be it.

Because we were so tired of the Northeast cold, my husband and I chose Miami because of the warm climate. Mahoney, Hadlow & Valdes-Fauli, the law firm that I started with, was only about thirty attorneys, but it was the branch office of the oldest law firm in Florida, and it hired me to work in its litigation department.

Miami was a wonderful city for a young professional. And I credit this firm for nurturing me and giving me the start I needed to become the trial attorney I eventually became.

Black: When did you realize that you had accomplished what you needed to in Miami?

Arguello: My husband and I wanted to start a family. We wanted our children to know their grandparents and aunts and uncles, so we decided to move back to home to Colorado. By this time, I had five years' experience and a number of trials under my belt, which I felt was enough experience to allow me to go out on my own, if the Colorado law firms still had doubts about my trial abilities.

Fortunately, that did not come to pass. I joined the law firm of Holland & Hart, which at the time was the largest law firm in the Rocky Mountain region. Like most other law firm associates, my goal was to make partner. Once again, I put my nose to the grindstone and I worked hard.

Black: Did the hard work accomplish what you intended?

Arguello: My second "aha" moment came about because, as I became familiar with the internal politics of such a huge firm, I realized that I was at somewhat of a disadvantage because I was in a small regional office. I intuitively sensed that hard work alone was not going to ensure that I made partner, unless I had a huge book of business, which would not come easy because of my location in Colorado Springs.

So as I thought through my situation, I realized that I needed to find the most respected and influential partner in my office and make myself indispensable to him. Yes, at that time the partners were all male.

Black: Did that turn out to be the right plan of action?

Arguello: At the time, I did not even know that the person I was looking for would come to be commonly known as a mentor, someone I could trust, someone who would provide me some protection from the in-house politics and who would help me develop the competencies that would lead to partnership. So I looked around the firm for such a partner, but also someone with whom I had a natural rapport. I sought out projects from him and soon I was handling the work for the bulk of his clients, and I took exceptional care of his clients. I made sure he always knew the status of his cases. I consulted him for major decisions, but did not bother him with the little stuff. In return, he served as counselor, advisor, and mentor to me.

Black: You didn't wait for a mentor to find you, did you?

Arguello: You need to be assertive and find and recruit a mentor who not only has influence, but who also has an excellent reputation and who exhibits the qualities of professionalism that you want to emulate.

I finally grasped the brass ring; I made partner and became head of the litigation section of the Colorado Springs office of Holland and Hart. I was now a respected partner in my firm and I was able to impact my community by being the youngest person ever elected to the Colorado Springs District 11 School Board. I was making more money than I ever dreamed was possible, but for reasons I did not understand, I became restless. I stopped rolling out of bed in the morning excited about going into work. I really thought there was something wrong with me. I should have been on cloud nine, and instead I was dragging my feet.

Black: Judge, you had accomplished more than most people do in a lifetime, so what was at the core of your discontent?

Arguello: So I went to see an employment counselor. Talking to him, I realized my third "aha" moment. It is really important to understand who you are and what makes you tick. He helped me to see that not only am I a type-A personality, who is very competitive, but also I am a goal-oriented person who constantly needs to be challenged. So once I made partner, my goal was accomplished.

Black: That was a pretty big insight. Was there more?

Arguello: What I loved about being a lawyer was the research and problem solving. As a partner, with the high billing rate, much of the work I loved about being a lawyer had to be delegated to younger lawyers. Add to that that I had two young children and my work hours did not allow me to spend as much time with them as I wanted and they needed.

My son drove that point home one night when I was reading to him and he described the kangaroo with a baby in the pouch as a daddy kangaroo with a baby kangaroo. It had never occurred to me that was anything other than a mother kangaroo, and I couldn't leave his description unexplained, so I asked him, "How do you know that is not the mommy kangaroo?"

He very sadly shook his head and said, "No, mommy kangaroo is working."

After I put him to bed, I cried myself to sleep and decided it was time to make a major change in my life, or one day I would regret it. I would turn around and my son would be graduating high school and heading off to college and we would not really know each other, so I decided to scale and dive off a new cliff.

Black: What cliff was that?

Arguello: The cliff I chose to scale was academia. I love to teach, and I am a good mentor. I also figured that if I could write briefs to the Colorado Supreme Court, I could surely write a few law review articles.

Again, I had hoped to be able to stay in Colorado. Fortunately, I got some wise counsel from another professor who advised that I needed to pursue a nationwide search for teaching positions, because the Colorado schools would not think I was prestigious enough, despite my Harvard Law School degree and my partnership in a major law firm. And she was correct.

I chose the University of Kansas (KU) because it was only ten hours from Colorado by car and the faculty at the University of Kansas rolled out the red carpet for me with letters, phone calls, and email messages. They also told me my teaching package would be overseeing the trial advocacy program, teaching contracts and bankruptcy law—the three areas of the law that I was most experienced in and interested in teaching.

Now, teaching is the only job I have ever had where they paid me and gave me money to hire research assistants to help me research issues that I chose to try to solve, not issues that my clients or others chose for me. It also allowed me to mentor and nurture so many students on their journey through law school.

As usual, I dedicated myself to being the best law professor I could be. I was honored with the most prestigious teaching award given by KU, the William T. Kemper Fellowship for teaching excellence, and I accomplished my goal of gaining tenure and being promoted to full professor.

I absolutely loved teaching at KU. And Lawrence, Kansas, was the perfect community in which to raise children. But Kansas was not home, and our parents were getting older and having health issues, so we decided that it was time to return back home to Colorado.

Black: Was that a difficult move, professionally?

Arguello: I feel blessed, because it seems to me that God has always watched out for me and has provided for me when I needed something. In 1998, another lawyer with whom I was acquainted, Ken Salazar, became the first Latino in Colorado to win a statewide election as attorney general.

Ken called me and offered me the job of deputy for state services in the attorney general's office. I accepted his offer, and two weeks later, found myself back home, doing incredibly challenging work on behalf of the people of Colorado. The work I did in the AG's office was some of the most satisfying legal work I have ever done. I was able to practice law again, arguing cases in the Colorado Supreme Court and the Tenth Circuit Court of Appeals. The work we did in the AG's office actually improved life for and protected the people of the state of Colorado.

Black: When did you set your goal to become a judge?

Arguello: I didn't even think about becoming a United States district court judge until I was forty-two years old. I just wanted to be the best lawyer and best professor I could be. I was in my mid-forties the first time my name was sent up for a federal appointment. Politics intervened and my nomination never saw the light of day with the Senate. It took me eight years to get to the federal court bench after that.

People often ask me how I handled the uncertainty. My response is that if it is part of God's greater plan for my life, it will be. If it is not, then it will not be. In the meantime, I just moved on with my life.

I became a partner in another major Colorado law firm, Davis, Graham & Stubbs, and then took a leave of absence from that job to become in-house counsel to my undergraduate alma mater, the University of Colorado at Boulder. I wouldn't trade either of those experiences for anything.

Black: How would you summarize the lessons of your journey?

Arguello: Unfortunately, many people stay in situations in which they are unhappy and unfulfilled, merely because they are afraid of change. I have never been afraid of change.

As a matter of fact, I thrive on change. It energizes me. I am able to give a hundred percent effort because, believe it or not, even at my age, I still roll out of bed every morning excited about what my workday has in store for me. Whenever I get to the point that I am no longer excited and challenged, then I know it is time to move on.

It is impossible to work at your full potential if you are just going through the motions because you need a paycheck, and life is just too short to spend it working a job you are not excited about.

I came from such a poor background that when I was in law school, I remember listening to my classmates in my ethics class discussing their goal of earning hundreds of thousands of dollars in practice. I thought that was obscene. But the point is that I've never let money be the deciding factor in whether I took a job. For example, when I decided to become a law professor, KU was actually the lowest monetary offer I received. But I chose Kansas because I just felt it was the right fit for me.

I knew that the faculty was not going to sit back and see if I was good enough and if I could make it. Rather, the faculty was going to do everything it could to ensure that I was successful as an academic. And they did, and I was!

When Salazar offered me a job in his administration, I asked him what the pay was. He said, $75,000. Keep in mind that by this time, I had been practicing quite successfully for almost nineteen years. And now I was going to be making less than a first-year associate in a big law firm?

In fact, my son, who by this time was thirteen years old and did not want to leave Kansas, stated it very well in his arguments to me over the move. "Mom, how does it make sense for you to uproot the whole the family to take a twelve-month job that pays you less than your nine-month teaching job at KU?" Well, he had a point.

If I had not taken that huge pay cut and worked side by side with Senator Salazar for four years, he would not have discovered that I was a very talented, hard-working lawyer whom he could wholeheartedly fight for and support for a federal judgeship.

Black: You are now at the pinnacle of your legal career. What do you see?

Arguello: So I have had an exceptional legal career, and here I sit at the pinnacle of that career, a United States district court judge with lifetime tenure. I love being a trial court judge. I have now been a federal district court judge for more years than I have ever stayed on any other job. And even after all these years, I find the work challenging and satisfying. There is no question in my mind that I will stay with this job until I'm old enough to retire or take senior status.

But in the meantime, I began wondering whether there were other cliffs I could scale and dive off, without having to leave this job, which I love. I found that there were, and that scaling this cliff makes me more fulfilled as a person—not as a lawyer, as a contributing member of society. I believe that we all have an obligation to reach back and do what we can to help others scale their cliffs by mentoring, opening doors, helping to train them, networking them. That is one of the reasons I spend so much time mentoring other lawyers. And more recently, creating a nonprofit called *Law School... Yes We Can*.

I remember when I thought success was winning a case at trial, or making partner in my law firm. And those are not bad things to strive for, but as I've gotten older, and gained some wisdom, the meaning of success has changed for me.

"Success. To laugh often and much. To win the respect of intelligent people and the affection of children. To earn the appreciation of honest critics and endure the betrayal of false friends. To appreciate beauty. To find the best in others. To leave the world a bit better, whether by a healthy child, a garden patch, or a redeemed social condition. To know even one life has breathed easier because you have lived. This is to have succeeded."

The beautiful words of Ralph Waldo Emerson and the inspiring lessons from the amazing journey of Federal Judge Christine Arguello. Judge Arguello's story illustrates: Learn to thrive on change. Focus with all your being on the position you have, squeeze every ounce of experience out of it, and when you're complete, decide to scale and dive off a new cliff.

When you find a door is closed to you, find a window and climb on in, as Judge Arguello did so many times. Find a mentor, or seek the wisdom you need to help you see the situation as clearly as possible. If there is a need, fill it. Just as she did, by starting *Law School...Yes We Can*.

And most importantly, she shows us to never let fear or lack of experience hold you back.

Dr. Joseph Ramos shows you what can happen if you dream big—I mean really big! He is a physician, a professor, a pilot, and an attorney.

Dr. Joseph Ramos
Personal injury attorney and medical doctor

" I began to ask, is this really what I want to be doing? Is this really all there is?"

Black: Dr. Ramos, your journey is certainly a zigzag path. When did that feeling of wanting more hit you?

Ramos: I remember that very well, because there was a time when I had been practicing medicine for about ten years. I was an associate clinical professor at the University of Colorado. I was on the admissions committee. I had a job that was one that people would love, as a physician—level-one trauma center, teaching some of the best of the best in a very competitive residency, a very competitive medical school—and I remember feeling like there was just something missing.

As part of dealing with that feeling of something missing, I started doing things such as testifying as an expert. At the university hospital, attendings serve as experts, because everyone over there has pretty CVs and has written papers and done things like that.

Black: So what did you do?

Ramos: I started serving as an expert. I thought that might be an area where I found more satisfaction in life. In no time at all, I had served probably in over a hundred cases in some capacity or another, either via testimony or reports or opinions, and it still was not quite doing it for me.

And so I was at a point in life where I started to feel like if I was home for a holiday or working at night away from my family, I'd begin to question: Is this really what I want to be doing? Is this really all there is?

And it was at this time that I realized that what I loved in life was I loved teaching—I loved learning. But I didn't feeling like I was getting either of those in this situation.

And it may go back to how I was raised. I'm the oldest of eight biological children and ten children that my parents raised. I came from a small town. When I would go home, people looked at me as if I was the one who had made it—I was the one who had gotten out of there.

There was this sense of accomplishment on the outside, the way people looked at me, but not a sense of accomplishment on the inside. And it was at that point that I had my "aha" moment.

My "aha" moment came when one of the things I had reached out to do, as I mentioned, was this expert work.

Black: What did that expert work teach you?

Ramos: Always spread your wings and always try to learn more, because the smallest thing may be actually your ticket to something big. It seems like writing an expert report or giving expert opinion, in light of being a professor and being on the admissions committee and doing all these other things—it may seem like that's a very small thing, but it actually opened the doors to much bigger things for me.

I had provided expert testimony a particular day in court. And my wife knew that I loved doing this testimony; she knew I really enjoyed my days when I went away to do that. And I came home and she asked me, "Hey, how'd it go today?" And I said, "Ah, it was all right, it wasn't great."

She could sense just this disappointment in me, and she said, "Well, why, what happened?" and I explained to her a little bit of the case and told her how I didn't feel like the person's story was told. They were going through this emotional trauma of even going to court for a reason. And I very much wanted to make sure that everyone knew the reasons behind that. And they can make their own judgments on what's right and wrong, but I didn't feel like that story had been told.

And so I related that in that way to my wife and she said, "Yeah, I understand, and you know, that is disappointing."

And I made the statement to her, I said, "You know, they're lucky I'm not an attorney, because if I was, they could run, but they couldn't hide."

And that "aha" moment of saying, "They're lucky I'm not an attorney, because they could run but they couldn't hide," really set the foundation up and changed the rest of my life in a very, very positive way, in a way that I can't tell you how much satisfaction I get from each and every day getting up.

My wife teases me because I whistle in the shower at four in the morning.

Black: Before coffee? Now that's happy. So what was next?

Ramos: I started law school. And that old saying that you can look at the glass as half full or half empty is very, very, very true. I always looked at this as a blessing, this opportunity to go to school again and to learn something.

So I worked full time through law school. I scheduled shifts around law school. I enjoyed the Socratic method where they call you out, making you stand up and answer questions. And I had been doing that to residents for years, and so frequently I felt like it was "Ask a Doctor" moment throughout law school. I was continually getting called out and standing up and answering questions, and what I realized quickly was that where attorneys couldn't wade out into deep water and swim — like I had experienced that time in court — I could. I could get out in the deep waters in any of these conversations and I could still swim, because I had another body of knowledge, and I could incorporate that and I could find a way to do that and enjoy it.

Black: What was your first experience in a law firm like? Was it what you expected?

Ramos: I'd done an internship, actually, at a major firm in town, where they practice almost exclusively medical malpractice. And my knowledge, well, I realized it was front and center in everything we were doing. And in fact, there were times when they would do depositions and they would set me in another room and they would live scribe through to me what the doctors were saying and I would be messaging back the attorney at the table the things to ask and the things to go after, and this is while I was an intern. This is before I had even completed law school. And I began to realize that my knowledge would be front and center because of my background in medicine.

The surprising thing and the disappointing thing at that point that I realized was that my value system wasn't always put forward in many situations. There would be cases where, for example, I didn't necessarily agree with going after a physician on a particular issue, but it became about winning and not necessarily about values. And I understood that that's not where my happiness was going to be.

I was offered a job there at the completion of my internship, and I turned it down and I got a law partner and I opened up my own firm.

At this point, I'd already made a mark on the community with expert testimony. I had a partner that was probably at the top of the legal field in Denver, and he had a reputation in town as being "The

Guy." And all of a sudden, I found my name on the side of a building with his in very short order. The practice was a screaming success. We had more business than we knew what to do with. And we were practicing excellent law. I was learning every day and there was still something missing.

Believe it or not, there was still something missing.

And again, it was values, personal values. I began to feel like it was about the value of the case and not the value of people. And we talked about people like they were cases: "No, don't take that case, it's not worth anything," "Oh, that's a big case, you know," do X, Y, and Z, and everything was case, case, case.

Black: How did this make you feel?

Ramos: I was so unhappy, because the one thing, going back to my medical experience, that I absolutely love is—because I still practice medicine and I love being able to treat people. And it doesn't matter if you come in and you're a multimillionaire or if you are homeless—if you need care, you get it. And I have found a great deal of satisfaction in doing that over my medical career, and I wasn't finding that in my legal career.

So I had my name on the side of a building. I had my name on the letterhead. I was making incredible money, but I wasn't happy.

Black: What was the straw that broke the camel's back?

Ramos: We'd just had a wonderful day in the firm, we'd had a $650,000 day. I remember specifically. We had a couple cases that had settled in the same day, one for $250,000, one for $400,000, one at trial and one in a mediation just prior to trial, practically on the courthouse steps. And I remember my law partner saying, "Let's go celebrate!"

And I remember thinking, I would only celebrate if I could get out of this situation. And I went home and told my wife that. She said to me, if this doesn't fit with your values, why are you doing it? Her words hit me in the heart. And I'll never forget that.

Because it's so true, if it doesn't fit with your values, why are you in it? We were comfortable financially. We weren't wealthy, but we were comfortable. Why am I doing this? Is it for money?

Black: So what did you do?

Ramos: I left that law partnership, and it was the best thing. And the ride since that time has been so incredible. It's been so filled with happiness, because every decision I make is based on my values.

I got tired of hearing in my prior firm, "We're not here to help everyone." And I started my new firm with the perspective of, "We are here to help everyone." And I hired people who I felt based their core values in Christ.

Now, I know that not everybody has a, maybe, religious perspective like I do, but it doesn't matter. You have to draw your values from somewhere, and so I looked for people who—whatever their religious values were, didn't matter to me—but their core values had to be in those things: love, peace, patience, gentleness, kindness, a desire to help. Because you can't help in every case. Let's be realistic here. But that they looked for solutions—they tried to the nth degree before they said, "I can't help."

And I started to look for people like that. I hired people from medical offices. I hired people who had been injured before. I hired people who came from service industries. I didn't hire people who had been on law review. I didn't hire people who were just getting picked because they had some accolade after their name.

I hired people who had an accolade, if you want to term it that way, in their heart. Where was their value system for caring for people? If they made me better than I am. And then I made them better than they were and there was this building that began to occur.

Black: How does focusing on values and surrounding yourself with like-minded people impact your life today?

Ramos: I run one of the most successful personal injury firms in Colorado, I have no doubt about that. I have a team that handles business personally with love, with so much love that our clients don't even realize how busy we are. And that is the ultimate feeling of success: when you're busy and you're successful, but the people around you don't sense that stress. The reason is because I demanded love and I demanded quality and I surrounded myself by people who demand the same and who care, and it's a joy to walk in here every single day. When you take that full circle—you know, I would imagine people go, "Look, this isn't realistic, helping everybody," and what I can tell you is dream big, because it's much, much bigger and it's much more successful than you ever even imagined.

Black: Do you have pearls of wisdom you'd like to share?

Ramos: That first and foremost one for me is, remember to be thankful. Never forget where you've come from. Remember that when you think you have a problem, it's probably what I would call a first-world problem. Your car won't start. Well, thankfully we live in a country where we expect to have cars. What a first-world problem! Be so thankful that you have a car that won't start, because it could be so much worse—so, so much worse.

I tell my staff frequently here, when they feel pressed on a deadline, we have realistic problems like any law firm, you know, a deadline coming up or a difficult witness or an expert that won't communicate with us or a report that somebody didn't get us. But whenever that comes up, I go back to all those days and nights in the hospital and I go to my staff and I say, "Hold on, is anybody dying around here?"

Because it was rare in a level-one trauma center for all those years that I had a day where somebody didn't die. No one is dying around here. And when you put it in perspective, when you remember to be thankful for your unanswered prayers, when you remember that really we kind of have a higher power that's protecting us from our impatience, it will make every day a lot better. So that's the first thing.

The second thing I would say is, always dream big. We are so limited by our own perceptions. When you realize that we use—I've heard—less than one percent of our brains, it's certainly less than ten percent of our brains. When you realize how much potential you really have when dreams start to happen and you realign, and then the dream is bigger, and you realign, and then the dream is bigger, you realize how low you've actually set your standards. I think we do that because we let small negative events influence our ways of dreaming.

Joel Osteen—one of his great sayings is, "A setback is a good reason for a comeback." And I will tell you that if we dream bigger, you'll realize that you have less setbacks because you'll always be striving for higher. By setting my goals big and by dreaming big, things have happened for me that I never dreamed of.

And the third piece of advice I would give people, and it's kind of the basis of everything I've just said, and that is, I'd make all of your decisions based on your value system. Make every single decision based on your value system. And if you don't know what your value system is, just stop. Just sit down with the people you love, have that quiet moment. For me, it's maybe a quiet moment of prayer or a conversation with my wife. But identify your value system.

And you will know inside when you're in line with your value system. Only you will know. And when you identify what that is, don't do anything less, because if you do, you'll be unhappy and unfulfilled. I was that way when I was a named partner in a major, successful firm—as I said, the dream scenario. I was unfulfilled, unhappy, because my value system wasn't being fulfilled.

And now I look back and I also realize that when I was in that system, I wasn't reaching my fullest potential. And if you work towards your values at all times, you reach your fullest potential, because you'll continue to strive until you are there.

Let the lines that you draw in the sand be value-based and let them have meaning. And don't draw any lines in the sand until that's what they're based on.

Black: Dr. Ramos, those are great pearls of wisdom. Now, do you have any parting words?

Ramos: Hard work beats talent every day. It's a principle that I've lived by. I came from hard, hard working parents and I saw that value. I learned that value, and there is no doubt along the way that things have happened in my life where there were much more talented people, but I outworked them. So hard work beats talent every day.

Dr. Ramos' story reminds us to take responsibility for the happiness and joy in our life. And ask yourself, if something doesn't fit with your values, why are you doing it?

Dream and dream big. You are only limited by your own perceptions.

Always spread your wings to learn more. Sometimes, the smallest thing can be your ticket to something big.

Chapter Two

Find Your North Star

Have you ever stopped to think about what fuels you? What guides you? Why you're on the planet? Or the mark you want to leave on your family, friends, profession or community?

I will go out on a limb and say you probably haven't given it much thought. Because life keeps happening month after month, year after year.

Let me ask you: are you content with your life? If not, I would recommend that you stop and take the time to look inward and find what really fuels you. Think about what gives you joy and lights your fire.

Most people spend more time planning vacations than planning their lives. Does that ring true for you? So carve out time to think. I assure you that if you're honest with yourself, you will find your North Star, just like lawyers Maia Aron and Denver Doxilly.

You will be inspired by their passion and single-minded focus to find their calling.

Maia Aron works on high-profile complex litigation cases—her dream job. Yet something was gnawing at her.

Maia Aron
Associate in Kozyak Tropin & Throckmorton's complex litigation department

"*But the practice of law, while challenging and intellectually stimulating, did not by itself fulfill me as a person.*"

Black: Maia, take me back to the beginning.

Aron: To begin with, I moved from South America to Miami as a 16-year-old who spoke no English. As you know so well, Paula, I'm very driven.

Black: Yes, you are, Maia.

Aron: Despite the language obstacles, I worked hard, learned English, took the SATs, got a great score, and was accepted to the University of Miami. After graduating from UM Business School, I decided to stay at UM to pursue a law degree and an MBA in finance at the same time.

Black: Why was that important to you?

Aron: Because I always knew I wanted to be a commercial litigator. While in school, one of the things I loved so much was my involvement in student organizations in leadership positions. I was president and director of the two largest organizations in the school of business. I continued while in law school, where I served as the vice president of the Jewish Legal Society.

Black: Did you continue your community involvement once you started practicing law?

Aron: When I started practicing law, I decided to really focus on becoming a good lawyer.

Black: So what do you mean, Maia?

Aron: After working for two firms, I finally landed a job at the firm I always wanted to work at, doing what I always wanted to do: commercial litigation. But the practice of law, while challenging and intellectually stimulating, did not, by itself, fulfill me as a person.

After ten years, I came to understand that by focusing only on my legal work, I lost my essence. I felt empty. I was no longer the super-involved leader I had been in school. I missed my connections to my roots, the Jewish community.

When going to synagogue, I would feel an emotional emptiness. I also felt disappointed in myself. Something was calling me.

Black: So with this awareness, how did this help you see your life differently?

Aron: It wasn't clear immediately. The president of the local Jewish National Fund chapter happened to invite me to a breakfast with an Israeli ambassador. I went to the event and felt the spark. Here, I was presented with an opportunity to reconnect with my previous self. I saw no young professionals at the event, so at the end of the event, I decided this was my time to act.

I told the president I wanted to start the young leadership chapter of JNF. A couple of days later, we met for breakfast and we talked about our plans. By the end of the breakfast, the new chapter of JNF Miami, Young Professionals, was born, and I was the leader. A couple of months later, we had an event with 150 attendees—crazy! I continued to serve as president of this young leadership group for two more years.

Black: What happened as a result of being the president of JNF?

Aron: A lot of good things happened. I was invited to many events where I expanded my network beyond the imaginable. I was taken on a young leadership training mission to Israel. I formed relationships with two amazing mentors who are still in my life today, and they too are community leaders.

I made amazing friends along the way. And I was asked by two other Jewish organizations to be on their boards and to chair the young leadership group of one of them.

More importantly, I have reconnected with myself. I felt complete. At last, I was finally the person I always wanted to be. I was a community leader following in the footsteps of many of my family members. My grandfather would have been proud, because my service and involvement have grown exponentially.

Things kept coming my way. I was asked to be the regional president of the Miami chapter of the JNF. I have earned a reputation as a connector in the community and helped in ways I could never have foreseen. My profile was raised, not just in the Jewish community, but also in the legal community, which, by the way, was not the reason I did what I did. They have become positive byproducts of this process.

When people ask how I can do all that do, I tell them the truth—it comes from the heart. I'm blessed to have the opportunity to connect with my community. It's how I connect with myself and with my family legacy.

Black: What have you learned from your journey?

Aron: It has been surprising, exciting, and stimulating. I learned that I can be both an excellent lawyer, because I love what I do for a living, and I can serve my community, because it's the essence of who I am.

Black: So what does fulfillment mean to you now?

Aron: The practice of law, as good as it can be, can never completely fulfill me. I need to be active and help those that need my help. It is very important to have a life outside of work and connect with others. The connections raised my profile and allowed me to serve my community even better.

I learned that you should always take time to do things from the heart.

Black: Those are great insights. And I was fortunate to have been able to walk that path with you.

Aron: Thank you, Paula, for the part you played in helping me focus and making me realize that this was the path to finding my true self again. I'll always be thankful from the bottom of my heart. This was life-changing.

It was heart-lifting for me to watch Maia navigate this journey. Around every corner, she uncovered more and more connections that reinforced her commitment to this path.

Consider Maia's insights. Your profession can't be everything to you, just as no one person can be everything to you. You can struggle with the circumstances of your career or you can figure out what makes you happy and let that be the North Star that guides you.

The key is to focus on service. Ask yourself, what are the gifts and talents you are meant to share for the greater good?

I encourage you, find your North Star. When you're doing what you love and it fuels you, the unimaginable will happen.

Denver Doxilly is a contract specialist for the Department of Housing and Urban Development. He is a firm believer that no one knows the path that you need to follow more than you do, and we should all have the courage to follow that path.

Denver Doxilly
Contract Specialist for the Department of Housing and Urban Development

"*During my time in law school, I felt so much pressure from my peers to follow a more traditional path.*"

Black: Did you always think you would become a lawyer?

Doxilly: No, I didn't always think I would become a lawyer. To be honest, I always planned on going pre-med after high school, and that's exactly what I did. After about a year and a half of doing it, I knew it wasn't for me—but I had no idea what was. I felt lost, in a way, but I knew the direction I wanted my life to take. But to get there, I felt like I had to get away. And I decided to join the Air Force. I got stationed in California, and the base that I was at was receiving a new mission. So they're upgrading the infrastructure, but it was contractors completing the work. And I was able to work pretty closely with many of them and I learned a lot about the process that landed them the job, because it was a very, very large contract.

While I was there in the military, the Great Recession started and a lot of people tried to pressure me to stay in. I knew I didn't want to make a career out of it. I knew I wanted to finish school and continue on with a different career, but so many people thought I was crazy to want to leave something so secure in a time of such economic uncertainty. But I believed in myself. I knew what I wanted, and I wanted to go after it.

Black: When did you realize your true path?

Doxilly: Well, surprisingly, I realized my path during the military. It's like my work with the contractors and the contracting offices on base opened my eyes to a world of contracting I knew nothing about. I found out the US government is the largest purchaser of goods and services in the world, and that these goods and services are procured through contracts with small and large businesses, which in hindsight makes sense, because the work of the government—there's such a large amount to do, there's no way that it could be done by a government work force, so it has to be done through these contracts. And the ones that handle these contracts for the federal government are contract specialists and contracting officers. They ensure that these goods and services are procured in accordance with the Federal Acquisition Regulation, which is the FAR, which is just another code book as we're used to—you know, going through law school, different code books. And this one, as with all the others, requires a lot of legal interpretation and many of the skills we learn in law school.

I saw that this profession was very large, and provided great opportunities, but it had a reputation for being so hard to get into. And people would tell me, it's like, "Oh, not only is it hard to get into, but it's hard to progress through." So I tried to think of a better way to enter it that might help me progress even quicker.

That's when I decided I needed to go to law school and I decided to do that after I finished undergrad, because I thought maybe a law degree would put me on a fast track in this career field, even though a J.D. is not required for it.

Black: As you pursued this path, what did you learn along the way?

Doxilly: I went to law school knowing I wanted to start my career in this field, because I saw that it was a field with many opportunities where a legal background would be so beneficial, and it was somewhere where many people with a legal background were not entering. And, on top of that, it was considered an aging industry, because not enough young people are entering this field for all the people that are retiring.

Black: While you were in law school, were you excited about your goal?

Doxilly: Throughout my time in law school, I felt so much pressure from my peers to follow a more traditional path. I would hear: you need to get on law review, you need to try to be an editor, and you need to network as much as possible with the legal community.

Even though the networking never felt organic, I was told I need to hunt for those summer associate roles. It's like that was the only way to find success, and that's what I constantly heard. It was like, if you don't follow this, your chances of being successful, it's going to be so low. You have to do this.

You know, there were times when I was asked what I wanted to do and I would tell them, with hesitation, always, but my plans, they were constantly met with negative responses like, why are you here, don't you think you should be doing this instead? You know, so many people thought I was crazy. And after a while, I just learned maybe I just need to keep my mouth shut and not tell anyone my plan, because it's going to be met with negative responses and I'd rather not deal with that.

I struggled with the pressure, and at times, I questioned myself if I was doing the right thing based on what I was hearing from them.

Black: How did you cope with this negativity?

Doxilly: I was able to speak to one of my professors, and I told him what my plans were, that I didn't want to be an attorney right out of law school, and all the pressure I felt from my peers, and how it was making me feel. And he told me exactly what I needed to hear. His response was, "You act like that's not okay."

And, you know, no one had put it that way to me, and the second he put it that way to me, it made me realize, you're absolutely right! At the end of the night, that's when I realized, I don't have to pay attention to this pressure that I feel from them, you know. His suggestion to me was: they might be responding that way because of their own fears of failure and uncertainties for their future. How right he was when I think back to it, because we're always told that this predetermined course is the best way we'll find success. We all have to do this—all have to do the same thing.

But I realized it was okay for us to travel down different paths and we all should, in my opinion, follow different paths, because we all can't make it on the same path. There's not enough space, in my opinion, down the same path for all of us, but we should feel comfortable following our own.

Black: What does your life look like today?

Doxilly: Well, today, I'm a contract specialist in a position where I'm promoted yearly and I'll receive contracting officer status in a couple of years. Once I get that, I get a warrant that allows me to sign off on federal government contracts worth millions of dollars. And I truly enjoy what I do, because I see the direct impact that it has on so many lives and I get to give business to small businesses, which are the backbone of our economy.

And I get to work on contracts that ensure people have heat and running water and some that ensure they have a livable roof over their head. I get to negotiate contract prices with CEOs and company owners and use a host of the skills I learned through law school.

The field I'm in produces such highly visible results that are not always recognized until something bad happens, as in the case with Puerto Rico after Hurricane Maria. But that's a great example of what can happen in an emergency, and what can happen when the rules laid out in the floor are not followed.

Black: You mentioned that procurement is an aging profession; how are you using that to your advantage?

Doxilly: In my office, my colleagues are fifteen to forty years older than I am, and I get to learn from them daily, and it's something I truly enjoy. They always tell me that I'm one of the youngest in this career field and the youngest in the department. They respect my opinion. I'm valued, and to be honest, I truly enjoy working with them. We get along so well, and I've had no issues fitting in.

But the Denver climate, it causes some health issues for me, and I was told by my allergist that I might have to move to a better climate, a more favorable climate. And I was talking to my boss about this, and he offered to transfer me; that wasn't something I was aiming for. But I was telling him that I just needed to be in a more favorable climate, and moving would have to be in my future. And when he offered to transfer me I was so surprised, because, like I said, that was not what I was going for, but the fact that he offered made me feel very special.

Black: How has this field helped you to expand your world?

Doxilly: You know, being in this career field has opened more doors than I ever expected. I'm in constant contact with people throughout various areas of this industry and have endless opportunities to network with them organically and through an organization that brings contracting professionals together.

Like I stated earlier, about the networking that I would be told that I had to do in law school, it wasn't organic. And I'm a big proponent of organic networking, because forced networking—sometimes it doesn't feel good. It doesn't feel right, and you don't see the best version of that individual. Through organic networking you can connect so much easier, when it's not being forced.

Black: So what do you think the future holds for you?

Doxilly: I always looked at life like I'm playing chess over checkers. Some of the moves may not make sense. It's all about positioning, and in my opinion, life should always be about positioning. And this can be hard to remember when we're dealing with life's day-to-day pressures, but it's something I'm glad I've consistently reminded myself of. I know I'm not done on my journey, but, because of the moves I've made, I'm in such a better position that will continue to open doors for me.

If I ever left my role, there are so many things I can do with this knowledge that I'm amassing and the educational background that I have, that one of my goals one day is to do consulting work, which is so easy to do with what I'm gaining, and having my J.D.

And looking back at it, I'm truly so thankful I had the courage to follow the path that I felt would work for me. It wasn't easy by any means, but I'm more confident and I look forward to what the future holds, because it's only going up from here.

Denver Doxilly has found a unique field for an attorney and realized he had a passion for it, and truly found a North Star to guide his path. He didn't listen to the naysayers, who were many. And the best part of all? He values the wisdom of his elders, who have taken him under their wing, and I suspect they will be in his life for years to come, as any good mentor is.

Chapter Three

Are You Just Interested or Are You Committed?

Management expert Ken Blanchard once said, "There's a difference between interest and commitment. When you're interested in doing something, you do it only when it's convenient. When you're committed to something, you accept no excuses, only results."

Commitment isn't a matter of willpower. It's what wakes us up in the morning and calls us to action. It drives us to believe we can change the world.

So find your passion and commit to it. You don't have to know how in order to begin. The path will reveal itself and results will follow.

Just take the first step. Do the work. Do the research and listen to your gut. You'll rarely be a hundred percent sure it will work, but you can always be a hundred percent sure that doing nothing won't work.

What if things go wrong, you may ask? But what if things go right, and what if the course of your life is changed in unimaginable ways? Take a chance with unbridled commitment, just like Laura Reich and Judge Roberto Ramirez. They met doubt, complacency, and resistance, but didn't let that get in the way.

Have you ever had a feeling that vibrates in your gut over and over again? It's telling you there is more to life or you don't have to accept your situation, or there is something better waiting for you. Do you listen? Is it just an interesting thought or is it something you are committing to—a commitment to act?

Well, here are two lawyers that listened and made a commitment to act.

Laura Reich is a litigator, formerly with White & Case, who has discovered a life she couldn't even imagine a few years ago, and has a compelling story to tell.

Laura Reich
Principal at Reich Rodriguez, commercial litigator formerly with White & Case

" *What right did I have, with all that going for me, to want more? Didn't I realize, didn't I appreciate how many others would give their right arm for what I already had?"*

Reich: I was sitting on an airplane at approximately 33,000 feet in the air somewhere in the skies over Orlando, Florida. The captain came on the PA system to announce that we were about two hours out from La Guardia Airport in New York City, where the temperature was 45 degrees and the weather partially cloudy.

I had some time on my hands to think about the last couple years. I was sitting next to my best friend and now my law partner, Clarissa Rodriguez. Clarissa and I have gone on several business trips in the last couple of months. I set up my laptop and my noise-canceling headphones to do a little work over the in-flight Wi-Fi. Just the basics, really—send a few emails, work on a brief I planned to file, that sort of thing.

Next to me, Clarissa was typing up a list of people and firms to whom our brand new law firm, Reich Rodriguez P.A., should send holiday greetings and small gifts of gratitude. And I realized that even though I am and have always been stupidly afraid of flying, I was in that moment happy—more than happy, even—I was content.

Black: Wow. Explain how that feeling came about.

Reich: I have to go all the way back to September of 1995, when I was a 14-year-old ninth grader at St. Thomas Aquinas High School in Fort Lauderdale. Being a brainy, rather than a sporty, kid with a pretty serious tendency towards the dramatic, I quickly joined the speech and debate team, where I met another brainy kid. She was a year older than me, a sophomore, who already knew how to navigate the scary world of our Catholic high school.

Of course, that was Clarissa. And by the time she graduated and left for the University of Florida, where I would soon follow, Clarissa and I had spent a lot of time together. My high school scrapbook, which we recently found, is full of photos that we now find so embarrassing. We were so young, and our hair and clothes were in serious need of an upgrade.

We studied together. We practiced our debate pieces together. We survived the attention of overbearing teachers together, particularly one nun, but that's a whole different story. We shared hotel rooms. We played some truly remarkable pranks, but only on people who deserved it. And we traveled together. Somehow it seems right that we're still traveling together.

Clarissa and I stayed close in college and then went off to start our lives. I went to the University of Florida Law School, where I met my husband, William, and first jobs and homes and kids soon followed.

Black: So what was your first job like?

Reich: My first job out of law school was at the Miami office of an international law firm, in the disputes department. And like every other junior associate in a big law firm, I spent long hours researching and writing and drafting memos, and very occasionally going to court. Unlike every other associate in a big law firm, however, I had some truly exceptional mentors. First among them was an accomplished class-action defense lawyer who, among so many other things, really taught me how to be a lawyer.

Another mentor was a top-notch environmental attorney who taught me how to combine billable work with pro bono projects that I was passionate about.

And when a former Florida Supreme Court justice joined the firm in 2008, he introduced me to the world of appellate law and to arbitration, which I still practice today.

So many others there left their fingerprints on me, so that by the time I became a senior associate, I felt like there was nothing I couldn't do well or at least learn how to do well. I loved my work. I loved my coworkers. And I loved the environment.

Black: Well, it seemed as though you had it all. You had arrived.

Reich: It did seem that way. So what right did I have, with all that going for me, to want more? Didn't I realize, didn't I appreciate how many others would give their right arm for what I already had? I struggled with those questions for a long time before finding answers.

The firm offered professional coaching, which I took advantage of, with limited success. But as six years became seven years became eight years, I began to wonder whether the path the firm had laid out for me was really the path I wanted.

Finally, it was the same mentors who had taught me how to be a lawyer who helped me find my own path. They encouraged me and supported me when I decided that I wanted to be a lawyer like my dad and my grandfather had been. I wanted a practice of my own.

So just shy of my ten-year anniversary with the firm, with my mentors and my friends firmly in my corner, I left the Big Law world, with all of its indicators and trappings of success, for a new practice that was, for me anyway, an unknown.

I matched up with a friendly acquaintance, who had left Big Law life a few years before to start his own law firm, focusing on hospitality, real estate, and transactional work. My new partner was successful, hard-working and intensely focused. His goal was to build a boutique law firm leveraging the experience of former Big Law lawyers, and he wanted a litigation department that was co-equal in expertise and experience to his transactional and real estate practice. I came on board to build that department.

And my wonderful mentors from my prior firm, referred me my first cases on my own, which is certainly not the stereotype of a Big Law law firm partner.

Black: Wasn't that about the time we met?

Reich: Right. It was at the Dade County Bar Association conference on small firm practice management. I was immediately impressed, and I set up a time to meet with you to discuss strategies that I could use to build a litigation department. You helped me take what I'd learned and combine it with the resources I had, to envision the law firm I wanted to create.

I remember coming back to the office after one of our meetings and bursting into my partner's office to tell him what you and I had talked about. Among many other things, you gave me concrete ideas to help me take my next steps. You didn't just say, "Oh, you should get published to grow your practice, so go write something," like all my other coaches had told me.

Instead, you said, "Who do you want as clients? What publications are they reading? What topics will catch their attention? And how do you write on those topics to showcase your expertise but without inadvertently providing them with a how-to guide to handle their problems without hiring you?"

As the litigation department grew, I found I needed help, and I remember you asked me, "Who do you want to work with?" And I immediately said, "Clarissa Rodriguez."

By this time, Clarissa was also a lawyer with degrees in both the United States and Spain. She was board certified by the Florida Bar in international law, something that I am so proud of her for. And she was one of only sixty attorneys in Florida at the time with that designation and one of very few women. She was fluent in Spanish and Portuguese, like so many of my new clients, and most importantly, I knew her to be a talented and ethical attorney. I knew her well as a person. I knew she was a good person. She was also married and had a child, so I thought she might like working in the environment I was trying to foster.

So after almost two and a half years at the boutique firm, I started to feel the same wanting-more feeling, and this time I knew to listen. Clarissa and I began to talk about, and then actually visualize, owning a firm of our own. We could do the work we were passionate about—civil dispute resolution, international arbitration—without hearing a contrary word. And I could finally explore becoming an arbitrator.

We vowed we'd create a firm that we had always wanted to work for, taking the best of our past experiences and leaving everything else behind. But we honestly believed it would take months, maybe even years to get to where we wanted to be. Money would always be an issue, right? And would our clients come with us? We didn't know.

The practice areas we wanted to grow into would still be there in the future, right, so there was no real rush. Maybe in another couple of years, after we'd analyzed and probably overanalyzed everything again and again,we'd finally go for it.

Black: Do you remember what I told you?

Reich: You encouraged us not to wait. You showed us with actual numbers that we could do it and that we could do it now, not at some unknown future time. You reminded us that we would have your help and that we would be successful.

Leaving the boutique firm where I'd first found success on my own was a difficult decision, but I knew that the litigation practice there would be left in solid and capable hands. And I was learning what a gift it is to have a friend like Clarissa to start a business with. Someone that I trust and know completely. Someone I've trusted ever since we were only teenagers.

So in August 2017, we opened the doors of Reich Rodriguez P.A. Our firm is women-owned and -operated, which makes us very proud. And we look forward to working with talented women and men in the future. Most of our existing clients stuck with us, and we've been retained by a number of new clients. All of our clients are being well served, money is being made, and Clarissa and I are living lives better than ever.

You know, like most parents, our families are so important to us, and this new arrangement gives us the flexibility to be great moms and wives. No more sneaking out of the office in the afternoons to go to recitals or parent-teacher conferences or doctor's appointments. We never need to do that again. I understand now that we can do what we want, practice how we want, with the people we want, and be successful.

Black: So, Laura, it's been quite an incredible journey. So do you have any parting thoughts?

Reich: You know, Paula, you encouraged us to take that trip to New York and several previous trips to visit clients and meet some potential new clients. I remember, when we mentioned the possibility of the New York trip, you asked us why we hadn't booked it already. You knew us well enough to know that while we would certainly get a number of business things done on our trip, and hopefully create some new business too, we would also have an awfully good time together.

And we're doing it now. We're living the lives we want and building the law firm we imagined now, and not at some unknown, unspecified future time.

So I remember sitting on that flight to New York beginning the descent into La Guardia Airport, and the pilot came back on the PA system to let us know we'd arrive at our destination a little ahead of schedule, where the weather was now bright and sunny. And I thought, hey, it's a metaphor! Even though I knew he was talking about La Guardia Airport, he might as well have been talking about Clarissa and me. We're on our way to our destination a little earlier than expected, and the future looks bright.

Reich Rodriguez is off on a great journey. As Laura put it, it's a gift to practice in a true partnership with a good friend that you trust. That doesn't happen often, but when it does, grab the brass ring.

Do you want more? Imagine the possibilities. What have you always had the desire to do, and with whom? Listen to your gut, as Laura did. The reward could be a life.

Take the first step. The timing may never look right. In fact, it will always look scary. Trust your gut and commit. Live the life you want. Find the joy in your work and the harmony in your life.

Judge Roberto Ramirez illustrates that there isn't a path with clear directional signs—Turn left in fifty yards. You simply have to make the commitment to make a difference, and the universe will conspire in unimaginable ways for you to produce extraordinary results.

Judge Roberto Ramirez
*District Court Judge for
the 17th Judicial District of
Colorado*

"I didn't know it at the time, but it was at that moment that I found my passion, in the same way some people refer to what they do as a calling."

Black: Judge, tell me how your story began.

Ramirez: My family is not from the United States. We come from the state of Tamaulipas, Mexico. We were migrant farm workers working here in the US, and when I was born, I was fortunate enough by complete happenstance to have been born in America. And with that came some great opportunities—opportunities for education that others in my family simply did not have. And I took advantage of those opportunities. I studied; I worked really hard. I was fortunate enough to attend a university and then law school.

And then I decided to give back to the country that had given me so many opportunities. And for the last sixteen years of my life, I have worked toward the defense of this country as a lawyer and a military officer. My first six years were spent on active duty. And by the time that I finished with my active duty tour, I'd either prosecuted or defended clients in over ten countries around the world and in many states here in America.

In my last tour on active duty, I was a senior prosecutor traveling the country working on the military's most serious crimes—homicide, crimes against children, crimes against women. And being in uniform, proudly serving this country, and working with victims—that was my passion.

But I left active duty. I joined the Reserves. I bought a house. I found a civilian attorney job. I was working for a municipal government, and I drove to work at the same time every morning and I drove home from work at the same time every afternoon, day in, day out. I was representing people fighting about money. Nobody's life was on the line; freedom was no longer at stake.

I no longer had that same passion. I needed more out of my career. I needed a change. And I get it. I have lots of attorney friends who look to change as well, many of them because they want things—they want bigger houses and bigger cars and more money. But I needed something different to feel successful.

Black: How did you find what your soul was looking for?

Ramirez: On this one afternoon in late spring, I'm driving home and there's an accident on the road, so I had to take a different route. And I'm driving slowly near these fields. Produce pick season had just begun, and I see these kids—these immigrant children—picking lettuce, and I'm instantly taken back to my own childhood, picking watermelons, and I'm overtaken with emotion. I had to pull over in my too expensive, too comfortable SUV, and I sat in my vehicle and I cried.

What I knew that these young lives had in store for them—it was simply too much. I wanted to run out there. I wanted to speak with them about the importance of education to their futures, about how bad options and fast money were also in their future, and how I had seen it in my own family, knowing that the wrong decision could lead to prison.

I had so much to tell them. I had so much to share. And so I grabbed a buddy of mine that weekend and we drove out there again and we decided to provide them breakfast and just talk to them. Unfortunately, the landowner chased us out, and he ended up calling the sheriff on us for trespassing.

I didn't know it at the time, but it was at that moment that I found my passion. In the same way that some people refer to what they do as a calling, I knew that I had to do something. At the same time, I also knew that running away from a sheriff and trespassing was not the best approach. But I knew that I had to do something and I vowed to make a difference. And I knew that I had something to offer.

Black: What were the skills you brought to the situation and what did you do next?

Ramirez: I had a law degree and I spoke Spanish, and I knew legal Spanish, and I knew that those things coupled together could change lives. And it was right around this time that a small group of us decided to start what would ultimately become the Spanish Speaking Lawyers Committee of the Colorado Bar Association. Our mission was to pour our collective knowledge and resources together and to put them to use in a terribly underrepresented community.

We began in northern Colorado and we started this free legal clinic, where we saw this tremendous need for legal assistance in a place without enough attorneys to adequately help, and it's been running for eight years now.

We took over a free domestic violence clinic for Spanish-speaking victims. We helped with wage theft and employment-law-specific clinics. But we also knew that although the need would always be there, we needed to address some of the root issues regarding why the immigrant population gets taken advantage of.

Black: What were your findings?

Ramirez: Education in the true sense of the word, the importance of schooling to succeed in this country, but also education of rights. Immigrants here are typically only aware of the laws of their country and they do not know when they are being taken advantage of. They do not know that they have free legal assistance at their disposal.

Black: Judge, well that sounds like a problem that was too big for one person to tackle.

Ramirez: I was fortunate enough to meet a federal judge who also had a passion for education, and who had put together what is called the Dream Team. And what we would do is travel throughout the state speaking to both school-age children and their parents about the importance of education.

I saw a need for others to join me, not just my contemporaries who were already on the committee, but to bring up a next generation of lawyers to get involved. And it was because of this that I started the first and only Spanish-speaking mentoring program for law students that have a desire to help that population, either through their careers or as volunteers like me.

I'd found my calling, and I had no idea that it would have come with some unintended consequences. I became a leader in my community.

Black: In what way, Judge?

Ramirez: I was first asked to be the head of the Spanish Speaking Lawyers Committee of the state bar association. Then I was asked to be the head of the Education Committee, and then the head of the Pro Bono and Volunteer Committee of the state Hispanic Bar Association.

I've been asked to create and teach a course at law school in Spanish, dealing with the representation of the Spanish-speaking community. This course is one of the only ones of its type in the country.

I've worked with two Latin American countries to help change their system of justice. There are so many global immigration issues right now in Europe, I'm going to have the opportunity to collaborate with leaders there.

Black: So did you set out to accomplish those goals?

Ramirez: If I had known that these things were to have occurred, I certainly would not have believed it. Not because I think small, not because I don't have lofty goals, but simply because those things were not my goals.

My goal was to do good. My goal was to start a dialogue about immigrant rights and helping them through the legal process. Because if I had set those things to be my goals, I certainly do not think it would have been realistic.

Goals are incredibly important. High-reaching goals are necessary for success. However, when we are simply checking boxes in our pursuit to reach a goal, others are going to see through this. It is disingenuous. And that will be evident to those around you.

You will struggle. There will be obstacles. There will be failure. But if it's your passion, and you get to do it, then that, in and of itself, is success.

The judge's story makes it clear that sometimes taking a detour is exactly what is needed in order to find a true calling. When he made the commitment to helping immigrant children, he had no idea how it was to happen. The journey unfolded with each step that was taken.

He took inventory of his assets, big and small. What could he contribute that would forward the progress of his passion? His legal Spanish, military discipline and organizational skills, and most importantly, the memory of that immigrant kid picking watermelons in the fields of South Texas.

His goals were not his roadmap; his commitment was. He inspired those around him to join the journey. Judge Ramirez created a community of like-minded lawyers to move his passion forward in all sorts of inconceivable ways.

Find your passion. It will lead you to places unimaginable, just like it did for Judge Ramirez.

Chapter Four

Are You Pre-Programmed?

Are you pre-programmed? Yes, pre-programmed, with what you should do, with no room for what you want to do? Is your comfort zone killing you?

Has complacency set in? Are you just going through the motions? Is complacency sucking the oxygen out of your dreams, your courage, and your passion?

I have the great privilege to work with lawyers and I know all too well the answer to that question isn't good.

It doesn't have to be that way. The legal profession is a traditional one, and consequently, it tends to create traditional environments, procedures, and expectations. Yet there are lawyers who have broken the shackles of tradition. It takes guts to swim upstream. It takes courage to believe in yourself when you have little evidence that it will be successful. It takes wisdom to apply the skills you honed practicing law in a different way or another environment.

Whether you are looking to build your practice where you are, find a new firm, or start your own firm, move from public sector to private sector or vice versa, or just stop the madness, you can make it happen!

Candace Duff and Miko Brown have broken the shackles of tradition with guts, courage, and wisdom. You will be inspired by their journeys.

Candace Duff knew what she should do and knew it wasn't enough, but she found a way to do what she wanted to do and stepped out of her comfort zone. Candace Duff is a mediator, attorney, arbitrator, and a published novelist aka L.J. Taylor.

Candice Duff
Attorney, mediator, arbitrator, published novelist, and book writing coach

"*One day I asked myself, 'Is this what you want to do for the rest of your life?'*"

Black: Tell me about your early influences.

Duff: Well, I decided to become a lawyer when I was twelve years old. I went from visiting nurse to spy to lawyer. There weren't any lawyers in my family. I probably got the idea from TV and books. As a child, I was a voracious reader. I read all the books in my parents' collection, including quite a few inappropriate ones. I used to read twenty Harlequin romances a week, when I was in high school, much to the chagrin of my math teacher.

I always had a creative side, though. I loved to sing. I loved to write. I wrote poetry and song lyrics. There are even some of my poems in the high school yearbook. And I even tried to write a science fiction novel when I was thirteen years old. It has heavily based on Star Wars—back then Star Wars was hit really huge, so there's a hero, there's a princess and all.

Black: Did your family play a strong role in guiding you?

Duff: I had a very strict mother, and she stressed education. You know, if she knew you could get an A, you couldn't come back in that house with anything less than an A. She also stressed having a profession. You had to be a doctor, a lawyer, or an Indian chief. She didn't want to hear you wanted to be a mail person or a janitor.

She downplayed hobbies. Being a writer and being a singer—those were hobbies, those weren't professions to her. In fact, my mother had a beautiful voice herself. She sang like Nancy Wilson. And there were a few recording studios who had courted her, but she declined, because, you know, back then you just didn't do that. You raised your family, you finished nursing school. You didn't go off into the sunset to try to become a singer, and she taught us the same thing.

Black: Did college fuel your creative side?

Duff: After high school, I got into Vassar College. And Vassar College opened up a whole new world to me. It allowed me to explore my creative side. I was an actress in the Ebony Theater Ensemble. I was a singer in the gospel choir. I was even a dancer back then, although I couldn't do ballet to save my life.

After Vassar College, I went into law school, and I didn't write while I was in law school. In fact, I couldn't even read fiction books. In law school, all you read are legal tomes. You do so much reading it pretty much turns you off from reading anything else.

Black: So what happened after law school?

Duff: After I left law school, I ended up getting a job at Greenberg Traurig. And Greenberg Traurig is an international firm—top one hundred. And so while I was there, I focused on becoming the best lawyer that I could be, because there were so few African American lawyers in the firm that I really wanted to be a good example. Later in my career, I focused on making partner and I worked a million hours, and there wasn't time for anything else.

Black: Did you find any time to write?

Duff: I took a vacation every year and during my vacation I would go to writers' conferences. I really liked the Maui Writers Conference, because it was in Maui, so how could you go wrong with that?

And I would dream. I would dream of writing a book. And there were so many people there, so many writers there, I would get all this intellectual stimulation while I went and I would dream about writing a book, but I just never had the time.

Black: And how was the rest of your life moving along?

Duff: I made partner at Greenberg in 2001 and I said, now what? September 11th happened later that year and I realized I had no personal life at all. All I had done was work, and I was restless. I misinterpreted my restlessness as a desire to get married. So I accepted the first proposal that I got, and married the first man who asked me. My ex wasn't very supportive about writing. He told me that even if I became a bestselling author, I could never stop practicing law, because he wanted to make sure that money came in steady. Needless to say, that didn't last very long, and he and I were divorced two years later.

My sister became unable to care for my niece. I ended up raising a fifteen-month-old baby by myself.

Here I was, a professional woman—a single mother, suddenly—working at Greenberg with a fifteen-month-old baby. I'm surprised my niece is still alive!

I had no time to write. I had no time to go to writers' conferences and hone my craft. I had no time for anything but to work and take care of my niece.

Black: When did things start to change?

Duff: My first "aha" moment came two years later. My niece was reunited with my sister and I had become a construction law expert and I practiced primarily real estate litigation, representing developers, but then in 2007–2008, the market crashed. Banks weren't lending. Real estate wasn't being sold. Condos weren't turning over and suing developers. People who had differences in real estate and construction thought it was better to settle than to litigate the issues. The cranes had stopped.

Like so many other attorneys, I had to reinvent myself. So I started doing work that I wasn't in love with, and I did that for a while. Until one day I asked myself, is this what you want to do for the rest of your life? And the answer was no.

Black: I bet that was eye-opening. What did you want to do?

Duff: I had two dreams that I had kicked to the curb for the first fifteen years of my practice. I wanted to be a published novelist and I wanted to enter into public service, specifically I wanted to be a judge at the time. And I decided right then and there that I would start taking steps to make those dreams come true, to make that happen.

I started attending writers' conferences again, and I joined Romance Writers of America, and I downloaded every single writing seminar I could find. And I learned about something called National Novel Writing Month, where basically maniacs from all over the globe, including Kazakhstan, sign up on the website and they vow to write 50,000 words between November 1st and November 30th of every year. I did that. I began writing a novel a year until I had four manuscripts written, and then I researched agents and editors and I started sending out my work.

And, you know, Steven King, in his book on writing, says, if you're sending out your work to agents and editors, you need to be ready to paper your wall with rejections. Truer words were never spoken, because I got enough rejections to paper my walls. But over time, the rejection letters started getting nicer and nicer, and longer and longer, where they said we like this about your work, but you need to work on that, maybe character development, or we like the pacing in your work and we love the characters, but you need to work on something else. But I was impatient and I wanted it to happen sooner.

Black: What happened to the second dream, of public service?

Duff: I applied for several judicial positions in state and federal court, and there were times when I got really close. The governor even interviewed me once. But I was beat out by other worthy candidates who had been trying for years.

When the hiring freeze lifted in state and federal agencies after the downturn, I applied for public service positions at these government agencies. But they kind of wondered why, after twenty years of practicing in a big-time firm, I wanted to go there. They wondered whether I was looking to retire, and they had the ability to hire younger people at a lower cost, so I didn't get those jobs.

Black: When did the idea of becoming an author really take hold?

Duff: Finally, in 2013, after attending the San Francisco Writers Conference, where they had a lot of seminars on self-publishing, I took a good look at my life. My mother had just died the year before, half my life was gone, and I wasn't any closer to achieving my dream of becoming a published author.

I decided to move into an area of law that would give me more flexibility with my time, that would enable me to do work that I loved, and to pursue my dreams, to become a mediator and an arbitrator, and to self-publish my novels. As a result, in June 2014, Duff Law Mediation and Waterview Publishing were born.

I had a lot of hurdles I had to overcome, and some of those hurdles were internal. They were emotional. They were things that I believed, and they stopped me from—or they almost stopped me from—moving forward.

I believed that following my dreams was foolish—that I could never survive on my own. I was never a big business developer at Greenberg, and networking wasn't my most favorite activity. In fact, I'm actually kind of shy. You probably won't believe that, but I was afraid that if I left the institution at which I had spent my entire legal career, I would flounder and fail. Well, that didn't happen.

I also believed that I wasn't the greatest fiction writer. Agents liked my pitches, the rejection letters did get longer and more positive, but they didn't represent me, they didn't agree to represent me once they got my writing submissions, and that made me believe that I wasn't good enough. I now know that's not true. I also believed that my work wasn't mainstream enough to interest a broad audience.

Black: So what made you think that?

Duff: There was a time when I went to this San Francisco Writers Conference and I submitted the second book in my romantic suspense series, Dreams Differed, to a big-time editor. I pitched it to her. She told me—I was sitting at a table with ten other people—because my heroine was African American and coming out of jail in the first scene of the novel, that my book wasn't mainstream enough. She said, "Honey, the only people who want to read about black people getting out of jail in the first chapter of your book are the black people." That discouraged me, because I thought, "Oh, who am I going to sell my books to?"

My books weren't necessarily urban fiction, so I didn't think I would fit into any particular niche. Little did I know at the time, my book appealing to African American women was actually a great thing. I learned later that the biggest reader of romance, of all types of romance, is an African American woman. She was helping me figure out my market. I didn't realize that at the time; I thought she was just being negative—and maybe she was—but, hey!

I also believed that the only legitimate way to get published was through an agent and a traditional publishing house. You see, back then, self-publishing had a stigma to it. People were publishing in what they call vanity presses and vanity books, but self-publishing hadn't reached the heights that it's reached today. So I thought I was doing something that wouldn't be acceptable. But the bottom line is, self-publishing—that stigma is almost gone. And if you look at the bestseller list today, a large percentage of the books are self-published. And if they aren't self-published now, they started out that way, and then big presses snapped them up. It's now become a very viable way to go.

Black: So what have you learned along the way?

Duff: Now that I've been out on my own for a while, I've learned so much. And one of the biggest things that I've learned is that you'll never be happy until you take a chance and make an effort to follow your dreams. If you don't take a chance, you'll always be asking yourself what would have happened if I had taken a chance, if I had tried.

I haven't made a ton of money yet, but I have never been happier. I also learned that it's possible to pursue my dream of becoming a published author and make a living at the same time. I went from thinking I wasn't cut out to be a business developer to starting and running two businesses in two different industries that are slowly but surely starting to gain traction. I published books in several different media all over the world. My mediation and arbitration practice is growing every day. In fact, I just went ahead and sent out an estimate for a $15,000 arbitration and no one has even blinked an eye. That could have never happened two years ago.

Black: Describe your career as the author L.J. Taylor.

Duff: My first book, Just Dreams, has more than 65 reviews and 4.5 stars on Amazon. All of my books have good ratings on Amazon. And if you look at my reviews, they're pretty overwhelmingly positive.

I get emails from people all the time who have read and enjoyed my books. I even got an email from a woman who said she was going through a really horrible time in her life and that reading my books have helped her escape. If I can do that for somebody, then I'm doing the right thing.

My books are read by men and women—people from all races and all walks of life and countries all over the world buy them. They've been bought in Australia, South Africa, Europe, India, and they're on Amazon, iTunes, Kobo Books, and Nook. You can find them in any places where books are sold online. The stigma that used to be associated with self-publishing is pretty much gone.

Black: How would you describe your life today?

Duff: My life today is very different than it was back then, when I was at the firm. I've published three books over the past couple of years under my pen name, L.J. Taylor. I now have more control over my schedule and more time to write, and I've never been happier.

Candace leaves us with inspiring thoughts.

Ask yourself: Is this what I really want to do with my life? Challenge your beliefs, because sometimes you will find that you have outgrown them, and maybe they weren't valid to begin with.

Take every opportunity to hone your craft, no matter where it takes you. Not a bad gig, when it takes you to a writers' conference in Maui, right?

Listen to your gut; it's telling you something isn't right. Candace listened to her gut many times along her journey.

Rejection. Rejection doesn't mean stop what you're doing. Learn from it and find another way to proceed.

Take a chance. Does your thirteen-year-old self still have dreams that speak to you?

How could this profession you love so much feel so miserable? It's not what you thought it would be?

Sometimes you feel trapped? Trapped by a situation that is insurmountable—or is it?

That's where Miko Brown found herself—trapped. Miko is a seasoned trial attorney that faced her reality.

Miko Brown
Trial attorney at Davis Graham & Stubbs, defending high-profile companies in catastrophic personal injury lawsuits nationwide

"*This path took a terrible toll on me and my family. Not only was I unhappy, but I was spending more and more time and energy focusing on my firm instead of the people and legal practice I loved.*"

Black: Miko, it seems as though you had figured it all out, but what exactly was that?

Brown: So approximately one year after I moved home to Colorado following law school, I discovered a prestigious litigation boutique firm where I was determined to work one day. After applying multiple times, I finally got an offer as an associate at this firm in 2007. This firm became my home for the next ten years. It's where I grew up personally and professionally. I went from being a newlywed to becoming a mother of three. I went from an associate to a partner. I developed wonderful business relationships inside and outside of the firm. I learned how to be an excellent trial lawyer and community leader. I developed my own clients and ceased being dependent on senior lawyers for work. I started a women's leadership program.

In short, I was on cruise control and doing exactly what I thought I should be doing. But for some reason, I also found myself becoming increasingly unhappy for reasons that were inexplicable to me. The more I succeeded, the more pushback and resentment I started feeling from many of my colleagues. I felt as though the firm was no longer trying to lift me up. Instead, it was trying to silence and neutralize me.

In response to this new environment, I did what I thought I should do—be a good soldier, try to adapt, and try to fix the problem. But this path took a terrible toll on me and my family. Not only was I unhappy, but I was having to spend more and more time and energy focusing on my firm instead of the people and legal practice I loved.

Black: So where did you turn for answers?

Brown: In November 2016, I met with one of my non-firm mentors to solicit advice on how to make my existence at the firm better and to try to turn things around. To my surprise, he looked at me and said very bluntly, "You know you can leave if you're unhappy, right?"

This was my "aha" moment.

I had developed such tunnel vision over the past decade that it never occurred to me that I had choices and that there might be a better place for me to work, one where I didn't feel like I was constantly banging my head against a wall.

I immediately went home and spoke to my husband about what still seemed like a crazy idea, leaving my firm and starting a new adventure. But without giving it a second thought he said, "Of course you can leave—please do. You deserve better."

To my surprise, my friends said the exact same thing across the board. Everyone around me had been seeing a problem, and a solution, that I had been blind to.

Black: So what did you do to help you see things differently?

Brown: When I finally took a step back, I saw that my mentor, my husband, and my friends were right. I did have choices, and there was a way out of my fairly miserable existence. I didn't have to work at a firm where I couldn't be my true self and where I felt like I had a target on my back. I didn't have to work at a firm where there was no longer value alignment and where the time I spent away from my family no longer felt worth it. It was time to move on.

As soon as I made the decision to find a new job, I felt like a one-thousand-pound weight had been lifted from my shoulders. Multiple people in my life who didn't even know about my decision suddenly started commenting that I seemed like a new person, and that there was a levity about me that had been absent for a long time.

I finally saw the light at the end of the tunnel. I also saw this amazing group of men and women who had come into my life over the past decade, largely through my diversity inclusion effort, and became unwavering support who would not let me fail. They were committed to me, my success, and my happiness, and I couldn't let that energy and love go to waste.

Black: What did you learn in the process?

Brown: During this journey, I learned how important it is to get outside of your head, think outside of the box, and take risks. I also learned how important it is to steer your career in a manner that will give you choices.

Thankfully, I was taught early on to develop my own business so I'd be more valuable to the firm than the firm was to me. Because I took this advice seriously, I was able to leave my former firm when I was good and ready.

I also learned that you have to trust yourself and your capabilities. Change is scary, and I'm always cautious of grass-is-always-greener syndrome, but sometimes you have to trust your gut and take a leap of faith.

Black: So what does your world look like today?

Brown: Knock on wood, but my life today is wonderful. I'm now at a firm that shares my values and lets me be me. I get to work with the clients I want to work with, those who respect and value different opinions, those who care about diversity and female leadership, and those who give me the freedom to be creative and do the best job possible.

I've also proven to myself that I've grown up and I don't need the safety net that was my old firm. I'm more capable than I imagined. There's no question that being a trial lawyer is tough, particularly when you also have a husband and small children who want and need your time and attention. The mommy guilt can be overwhelming when I'm in my home office working on a Saturday and my kids think I'd rather be sitting in front of my computer than playing with them, but this new confidence and happiness has helped me mitigate the mommy guilt. When I work with clients I like, in an environment I like, the time away from my family isn't quite as painful.

I'm also a better wife, mother, and friend when I'm professionally fulfilled and happy. Now all the energy that I previously spent fighting the naysayers, I can spend on the people and programs that feed my soul.

Miko shows us that even if you can't see it clearly, you always have a choice. She reminds us that it's possible to outgrow your situation, and that it may be time to move on. Miko learned that having a book of business made her more marketable, and ultimately she trusted her gut.

Maybe it's time for you to take a good, long look at your situation. Take inventory of what you like and what is troubling you. If you can be honest, you will see the situation clearly and you can start crafting a strategy to move toward a better life, as Miko did.

Chapter Five

Define Your Own Success and Tell Fear to Take a Hike

How to define success? The only person that can answer that question is you.

Every single person is different. Every lawyer has had different experiences and every lawyer has different needs.

So what is success to you? Is it money, position, title, meaningful work, time or flexibility? The list can go on and on and on.

But does fear derail your drive to succeed? Yes, fear. Sometimes that little voice creeps in—but no, I can't do that, I don't know enough, I'm not good enough—that fear of inadequacy.

I was listening to an interview with Alan Dershowitz. He confessed, "I don't fit in. I'm not as smart as people think I am. I still get nervous." Well, if Alan Dershowitz—the world-renowned professor, lawyer, and scholar—has fears, why wouldn't we mere mortals? It's not about the fear, that's a given. It's what we do in the face of it. It takes enormous courage to experience something new in the face of fear.

Lawyers Michelle Otero Valdes and Karen Lapekas share how they faced their fears and defined success in their own unique way. Their stories illustrate the importance of living your own story, not anyone else's.

Michelle Valdés chose a practice area that she found fascinating—all areas of it. The challenge? It's maritime law, and it's a man's world, just about every single aspect of it. But that didn't stop her one little bit.

Michelle Otero Valdés
Board-certified maritime attorney handling all aspects of admiralty and maritime law

"There were other women in the firm that wanted to kick the ladder out from under me because they think they need to do so to get ahead."

Black: What's the backstory that led you to maritime law?

Valdés: During my undergraduate years, it was the Reagan years. The thinking at the time was, if you graduated from college with a business degree, you'd be set.

However, after graduating from Florida International University with my degree in international business and management, I began working in banking at around the time that the savings and loan crisis was looming. Within a three-year period of time, I had been laid off from six different jobs in banking.

It was at my last job in banking that I decided I wanted more control over my destiny and not to be subject to the whims of an industry heavily regulated by government.

At this last job, I began assisting the government in essentially phasing out my own job and the jobs of many of my colleagues. It was at that time that I learned all about law school loans. I was tasked with assisting with the closure of the student-lending department of that bank and discovered that I could afford to go to law school. So I applied to law school and to my surprise, not only was I accepted, but I was also offered a merit scholarship.

By second year of law school, I had settled on wanting to practice international law. Arbitration was beginning to take hold in commercial matters, and as I had graduated with an international business degree, I had some working knowledge of these matters.

Because I wanted to focus my studies on international business, someone suggested I take the Admiralty I class, as it delved into numerous international law issues and as its practice was based in federal court.

That one class changed everything for me. I ended up booking that class, which meant I got the highest grade in the class. Because of that, my professor urged me to focus my future studies in this area. That professor also got me my first job as a law clerk for a well-known plaintiff's maritime firm, specializing in the injuries of crew and passengers aboard cruise ships.

I was a member of the International Moot Court Board and was preparing for oral argument. This preparation included having outside volunteer lawyers that would come in to judge the arguments and assist the students for competition. One of the last lawyers to assist me in my own preparation was a maritime lawyer who ultimately became my mentor and said, "If you ever need a job, give me a call."

By the time I graduated from law school, I had come to love maritime law and knew this is what I wanted to practice. However, little did I know that I still had a lot to overcome.

Black: But why maritime, given it's known as "a man's world" on steroids?

Valdés: While two years' time does not seem like a lot, it was, with law school loans looming, and perhaps a stubborn view on my part that if that is what I wanted to do, I'd find a way to do it.

The original plan was to continue working as a law clerk for that plaintiff's maritime law firm upon graduation and upon passing the bar, work as a first-year associate. However, just before graduation, I learned there was not an associate position available for me at that firm, and found myself without a job.

So after taking the bar, I knew I had law school loans to pay and a career to start, and I didn't want to sit idly by waiting for my bar results, so I found myself working as a paralegal for a civil defense firm floating from partner to partner, handling a variety of matters, including oil and gas franchise disputes, family law, real estate, and intellectual property, but no maritime law.

While working for this firm, I continued to interview at various maritime law firms, and while some simply said, "Call me back when you get your bar results," others discouraged me altogether from pursuing this area of the law. One well-known maritime lawyer even told me that I should go and practice family law, as maritime law simply wasn't suitable for women.

Undeterred, I received my passing bar results and called that maritime lawyer that gave me his business card a year and a half prior to that. He quickly scheduled an interview with his senior law partner, and a week later I was working for that maritime firm, Underwood, Karcher, Karcher & Anderson, P.A.

Black: And who were your mentors along the way?

Valdés: The maritime lawyer that assisted me while in law school and got me the job was Andy Anderson. He was the attorney that I reported to at Underwood, Karcher, Karcher & Anderson, and he taught me so much. There was another female lawyer at the firm that was practicing workers' compensation, and she was my direct report when Andy wasn't around.

When I showed an interest in Longshore and Harbor Workers' Compensation Act cases, she happily handed them over to me. Her name was Meg Kerr, and I learned a lot from her. Meg began handling workers' compensation cases about a year before I joined the firm, and she became so adept at handling these cases, she went on to become a Florida judge of compensation claims.

Meg would sometimes complain that only the men in the firm were getting the maritime law cases. Maybe Meg's quiet complaints to me made me stubbornly insist on handling maritime law cases. As the only other woman in the firm, am I destined to handle workers' compensation cases for the rest of my law career?

I did not want to be relegated to handling only workers' compensation cases at the firm.

Surprisingly, Underwood, Karcher, Karcher & Anderson made sure I did not suffer the same feelings Meg expressed of being seen as a second-class lawyer.

Black: How did you navigate various situations from position to position?

Valdés: I never feared moving from position to position, because it's my nature to ask lots of questions, and I made sure that the position I was looking at aligned with my career goals. For example, while I was still working at Underwood, Karcher, Karcher & Anderson, I was approached by Thomas Miller to work for them. I was concerned that this job would be a step back for my career, as I was now a three-plus-year associate and firmly entrenched in a good firm handling good maritime cases.

I spoke to numerous colleagues in the industry, including Andy Anderson, who by this time had left Underwood, Karcher, Karcher & Anderson for another firm, and they all encouraged me to take advantage of this opportunity. It was a very rare opportunity for a young attorney to work for an English P&I club.

At Thomas Miller, I handled every kind of maritime case, including collisions, pollution, cargo damage, general average, all forms of maritime personal injuries, maritime casualties, and maritime contract disputes.

However, by 2005, Thomas Miller was downsizing. I had two daughters, and while I was offered relocation to work in the New Jersey office, I once again had to decide how to navigate that next chapter of my professional career. Do I stay in marine insurance or do I return to private practice?

Once again, I turned to numerous colleagues in the industry to help me make that decision. I looked at my career goals, and the fact that I now had a family with small daughters going to good schools and making good friends. It was that soul-searching that had me return to private practice to work once again with Andy Anderson, this time as his law partner.

I was being scouted by several law firms, asking me to open up their admiralty law department or running their existing maritime law department. There were other women in the firm that wanted to kick the ladder out from under me, because they think they need to do so to get ahead—kind of a way to remove the competition.

That single situation in my life made up my mind: I would never kick the ladder when there is another woman looking to make it in this area of the law, and I will do everything in my power to help her succeed. In my mind, it is this belief that has made my law career in maritime law a successful and fulfilling one.

Black: What is your current situation?

Valdés: I am the managing partner of the Miami office of Chalos & Co. P.C., a well-known international law firm focusing primarily in admiralty and maritime law. This setup is ideal for me, as my daughters are now teenagers, and the freedom of being my own boss allows me to set up a situation where if one of my daughters needs to get homework done, she can walk over from school to my office and do it.

Black: So what did you learn about yourself as you progressed through your journey?

Valdés: What I've learned is that all of this talk—about assessing your life goals and making sure that they align with your career, and making sure we are practicing law with mindfulness—is not hokum. It is necessary to ensure that all the aspects of work, family, and home life are in sync.

I have also learned that if I put my mind and energy into something, it will come to a positive result. I envision myself running a maritime law office and having a good team to help me do it. That takes not only mindfully believing in yourself, but surrounding myself with people that believe in me too.

The key to entering a new circle is to assume you belong. Contribute in a meaningful way and be inclusive.

Michelle Valdés made her mark on maritime law. She was the first Latina to be board certified in Florida and the first Latina skipper of the Fort Lauderdale Mariner's Club. She has been president of the Florida chapter of the Women's International Shipping and Trading Association, USA, and has been on the National Sections and Divisions Council of the Federal Bar Association.

Why do I point this out? That is how you become relevant in a circle that doesn't look like you. Contribute in a meaningful way. Take action and lead. And remember, you can define your own success and tell fear to take a hike.

Karen Lapekas has faced her fears and redefined success in her own unique way. She's a former senior attorney for the IRS and now owns her own firm that focuses on IRS tax defense and litigation.

Karen Lapekas
Former Senior Attorney for the IRS now has her own law firm as an IRS tax defense attorney

"And why do we want to be society's version of successful? I think it's because we think it would make us happier. What if you could be happy without all the trappings?"

Black: Karen, I know you've been doing a great deal of introspection, would you like to share?

Lapekas: Many lawyers like myself are entrepreneurs. We traded the shackles of 40-to-60-hour-a-week jobs for the luxury of working 80 to 100 for ourselves.

We did it for a lot of reasons, one of which is the fact that owning a business is revered in our society. Our culture is founded on grit, ingenuity, risk taking, and wealth building.

But entrepreneurial life is not always glamorous. It not only costs us our time, but it comes at a much larger expense: our mental health.

I recently did a Google search and brought up these titles. The first was on Inc.com. The article was called "The Psychological Price of Entrepreneurship." Another was on Forbes.com, called "Depression Among Entrepreneurs Is an Epidemic Nobody Is Talking About."

Black: Was there a common theme in these articles?

Lapekas: A common theme among these two articles, and other ones I pulled up, is that the rigors of entrepreneurship lead to depression, and the legal profession attracts people more prone to depression in the first place.

You know what I hate about articles like these? It gives us one more thing to worry about: becoming depressed. Now we also have to worry about our mental health, too.

Black: So does that frustrate you?

Lapekas: Fortunately, I have a much different experience with entrepreneurship and depression. I credit owning my own law practice for being happy. And shouldn't I be? I mean, I have the ultimate dream job; I'm my own boss, I have the freedom to travel, decide my own hours, and write my own destiny.

Black: So you're living your dream, right?

Lapekas: Well, kind of.

Black: How so?

Lapekas: These things don't make me happy. However, I didn't start a law firm because I was searching for happiness. I started a law firm because I was running from depression.

Entrepreneurship was just one more of the many seemingly crazy risks I've made in my life, and I used to think I took risks to find happiness, from taking flying lessons and sleeping alone on the Appalachian Trail when I was only eighteen, jumping from an airplane on my thirty-second birthday, scuba diving shipwrecks at 120-foot depths at midnight, spending a month in China, studying for two different bar exams while working full time and using old books I found on eBay, biking two hundred miles in one day—hell—even going to law school. I used to think that taking risks made me happy. That adrenaline—getting out of my comfort zone—was my secret to success.

My old motto was, "If you're not living on the edge, you're taking up too much space." But I now know that I was not chasing adrenaline or taking risks to find happiness.

Black: So how do you see things differently now?

Lapekas: To be honest—embarrassingly honest—I was running from depression. I have fought depression for almost as long as I can remember. I say fought because I don't like to say I suffer from it. I suffered from it for years, but through suffering, I learned to fight it. I learned what made it tolerable. I learned what got me through it. I learned what made it lessen and lessen, until I could say I felt, well, normal.

When you fight the same opponent over and over, you learn its techniques. You know its second move as soon as you see its first. The fight thus becomes easier to bear. You don't fear it as much. And you can punch it out much quicker.

For me, depression is like that. I see signs of it very early, and I know what I need to do to avoid it spiraling out of control. Almost always, it requires me to do something, like breathe, or get out of bed, put one foot in front of the other, walk the dog, go out for coffee, go to the gym, call a friend, take a trip, jump from a plane, quit a job, start a business.

Black: Hmm, start a business?

Lapekas: Yes, even start a business. Six years ago, I had a great job with the IRS. I was a senior attorney litigating cases in the U.S. Tax Court. I loved it. It was great hands-on experience. I loved my colleagues and the benefits were generous.

But my shoulders started getting heavy as I walked into work every morning. It happened for weeks in a row. And one day I noticed that by the time I reached my office door at 7:30 a.m., all of the day's energy was already zapped. I started dreading Mondays again, which made me dread Sundays also.

My gut was talking to me. I was restless. I knew that the question I had to ask myself was not whether I could make enough money if I left, but whether I could be happy if I stayed.

And that question came down to this: Am I happy? And I knew that if the answer was no, I had to tell myself, okay, change it.

People ask me why I left such a great job with the IRS. I always give them the same reasons, like the salary was capped or I wanted a different challenge. It's funny; they ask me why I left, as if I had a choice.

I didn't know it at the time, but starting my own law firm was the greatest thing I have ever done to tackle depression.

Black: Wow, that's a pretty powerful statement. How could that be?

Lapekas: Well, necessity is the mother of change. As a business owner, I had to change. I can't afford to think negatively. If there is anything to this manifest-your-dream stuff, by God, I'm going to try it. I have nothing to lose, and it's free.

I can't afford to be an atheist. I've always had a deep faith, but it became even deeper, more of the spiritual but not religious type. I also can't afford to stay in bed all day, so I make sure to take care of my health. I have to get out of bed, go to the gym, and eat better. I can't afford to be comfortable. I have to get out of my element, meet people, speak, write, do new things, or I couldn't grow my business. I couldn't pay my bills.

Simply put, as an entrepreneur, I cannot afford to be unhappy. I'm on my own. There's no salary and no one else to pay the rent. If I don't make it, it means going back to a job where I might not be happy, and that is all the motivation I need.

In a sense, entrepreneurship for me has cured my depression, not created it.

Black: So you feel it has cured your depression, so to speak?

Lapekas: Perhaps the difference between me and someone who falls into depression through entrepreneurship is two things: I don't forget why I became an entrepreneur, and there is nothing more important to me than being happy.

Black: Do you ever feel that you're putting too much pressure on yourself?

Lapekas: Sometimes I fall into the thinking, I should be making more money by now; I should be doing more of this or that to grow my business; I should have saved more money. I should, I should, I should . . . And that kind of thinking is dangerous after a while. I start to feel like I'm failing to meet my full potential, that I'm not really successful. I can feel the downward spiral starting.

Black: Do you sometimes feel that you're just putting a smile on?

Lapekas: As business owners, many people greet us and ask, "How's business?" I have almost always answered this question, "Great, my bills are paid and I'm happy." I don't tell them I haven't saved enough for retirement, that I have huge student loans, or that I worry about having to ask my clients to pay.

Black: So what makes the difference?

Lapekas: I know why I started my own law firm—because I was unhappy, because I would do anything to avoid starting the downward spiral into depression, which I saw myself doing at my old job.

Everyone who has been through hell—and everyone has been through different versions of it—is more grateful for the little things. And I don't take things for granted. I don't take happiness for granted.

Black: I'm sure people look at you and your practice and envy your success, right?

Lapekas: You know what I think people envy, more than anything? Happiness. And why do we want to be society's version of successful? I think it's because we think it would make us happier.

What if you could be happy without all the trappings? For me, having fought depression and knowing such dark feelings for so long, the simple lack of depression is amazing.

Black: So what would you say to lawyer entrepreneurs that are struggling?

Lapekas: Don't get so lost in the messages we get as entrepreneurs that you forget why you're an entrepreneur in the first place.

Why did you take that risk? Was it really to get rich? Probably not. It's probably because you know that the ultimate success isn't money—it's happiness.

Waking up and not dreading the drive to work—that's success. Coming home, even if exhausted, yet feeling optimistic and energized for what's to come—that's success. Working on the weekends because it's what's right for your client, and not because the boss came into your office Friday afternoon and asked you to—that's success. Not having to ask permission to fly home when a family member is sick and you can leave within hours—that's success. Believing that you are now in a position to reach your highest potential—that's success.

When you feel like entrepreneurship is bringing you down, remember how it is bringing you up.

What a courageous story and powerful advice.

Karen has defined her own success. She stays focused and remembers why she is an entrepreneur. The endless should–should–shoulds don't stop her.

Karen is a fighter. And most importantly, she has done the soul-searching work to understand what she needs to do in order to keep moving forward.

Chapter Six

The Power to Be Happy

What does happiness mean to you?

There are many, many things that drive the feeling of happiness. We can experience happiness in our work, with our relationships, and with our progress towards achieving our goals. One thing I know is that if we don't feel some degree of happiness, it's very unsettling.

Yet I work with clients that do have good relationships, and they are progressing toward achieving their goals, and they like most aspects of their work. By all accounts, they should be happy, and yet they don't see themselves as happy.

Others are unhappy trying to achieve some level of happiness. And nothing seems to get them there. It's puzzling.

So I asked Dr. Elyse Hurtado, a professor at the University of Miami Department of Psychology, to help us understand.

Dr. Elyse Hurtado
Professor at the University of Miami, Department of Psychology

"Optimism is linked to longevity, life satisfaction, achievement, happiness, healthier relationships, even the ability to recover from illness and disease, but you have to truly be optimistic."

Black: What is the study of human happiness and positive psychology? Is it, "Be more optimistic and you'll be happier"?

Hurtado: Basically we're talking about life satisfaction—feeling good about your life and about yourself—what we call psychological well-being.

You've probably heard how important it is to be optimistic, the power of positive thinking. Not only that, but also how harmful negative thinking is to your health and to your psychological well-being. So yes, optimism is linked to longevity, life satisfaction, achievement, happiness, healthier relationships, even the ability to recover from illness and disease, but you have to truly be optimistic.

Black: I would think being more optimistic leads to being more grateful. So how does gratitude play into happiness?

Hurtado: Gratitude comes in two stages. First comes the acknowledgment of goodness in one's life—recognizing that we receive something that pleases us or gratifies us, and that life is good. Second is recognizing that some of the sources of this goodness lie outside the self.

The most interesting findings from the gratitude research are two things. First, that taking the focus off of the self and giving to others increases happiness and well-being. This is something we are finding over and over again in the research. And the second thing is that gratitude is a skill that can be developed. You can practice expressing gratitude.

One study, for example, found that people who express their gratitude are more willing to forgive and are more satisfied in their relationships. Another recent study found that keeping a gratitude journal improved physical and mental health outcomes.

Black: I would think at the core of happiness is relationships. We derive happiness from all sorts of levels of relationships, right?

Hurtado: Well, we've known for a long while now that relationships are fundamental and critical, not just to our emotional and personal lives, but also to our businesses and our professional lives.

What the research is telling us is a couple of things. First, it is not the quantity of social contacts or the number of events on our social calendar that is important, but rather whether a person's emotional needs are being met and whether a person feels someone will be there for them when they need them—something we call perceived availability.

The second interesting finding is that people get even more benefit, more of a sense of satisfaction and well-being, by being there for others than they do from, say, self-disclosure, or the sharing of one's personal feelings.

This would indicate that if you're feeling a little blue, instead of trying to get someone to be there for you, you should go out and do something nice for someone else—that's a nice way of looking at things.

Black: One of the things my clients struggle with is their achievements and their feelings of accomplishment around those achievements.

Hurtado: You, Paula, are probably more of an expert in this area than I am. I can tell you, though, what the idea is. First of all, you have to have ambition. Then you have to have realistic goals. And last, you have to put in the effort to achieve those goals.

To achieve a sense of satisfaction, meaning, and purpose in life, one should savor their accomplishments, strive for further achievements, and pursue success and mastery, both as a process and an end goal.

Black: Okay. Now that makes sense. So how does mindfulness play into all of this?

Hurtado: Mindfulness means attending to our experience—being in the present moment with acceptance.

People tend to think they are mindful because they have self-awareness and the ability to self-reflect, but really most people spend most of their time thinking about the past, replaying what has happened, and thinking about what they could have done or should have done, or they're thinking about the future, imagining what is coming. It's relatively unusual to just be in the present moment without judgment. And there's a lot of joy and happiness that people are missing in the here and now.

Mindfulness is a skill that can be learned and developed. And when it is learned, it opens up many possibilities for human happiness, developing strengths, being thankful, and finding meaning and purpose.

Black: So how do we take action and tap into the power to be happy?

Hurtado: Let us start with optimism. The research is clear—positive thinking and positive expectations lead to positive outcomes.

So do something nice with no strings attached. Make a list at the end of the day to reflect on your accomplishments. Then make a list to set up your goals for the next day. Make an effort to be more mindful, to be in the present moment with acceptance and without judgment. Take a moment to savor your coffee or your tea. Think about how it smells, how it tastes, and how the mug feels in your hands.

Be more grateful. It can be easier to think of things we do not have than to think of things we do. The truth is, the list is much longer of all the things we take for granted. We have so much to be grateful for.

Stop looking for the next best thing—for more and more. Stop and give thanks for what we have. What are you grateful for? Gratitude turns what we have into enough.

Dr. Hurtado teaches us that being optimistic, showing gratitude, nurturing good relationships, pursuing satisfying accomplishments, and being mindful are all key paths to happiness.

The good news is that Dr. Hurtado assures us that we can change our situation by applying her advice. The power to be happy is in your control.

Chapter Seven

You Can Do It Your Way

The legal profession has lots of assumed roles. Break the rules. You can grow your practice or chart a career path in any way that is right for you.

Yes, you can do it your way. And no, you can't sit in your office and will it into being.

It takes hard work and unwavering commitment. What will ignite your action?

Is it that you don't like the way your boss operates and you think you can do it better? Is it the feeling of being trapped? Is it because you see a need that no lawyer is filling? Or is it just in your DNA to do it your way?

You get to choose. Will you conform to the norm or will you create your own path?

Discover what could be possible if you step outside of what you know and embrace your capacity to bring forth an entirely new possibility.

You'll find inspiration from Joshua Hertz and Judge Alex Bokor. They created their own paths by not buying in to the conventional wisdom of the legal profession.

Joshua Hertz is a solo personal injury lawyer, a leader in the legal community, and a committed business owner who took the road less traveled.

Joshua Hertz
Founder of his own personal injury law firm, Hertz Law

"The bottom line is if you don't bring in business, you cannot be a lawyer working for yourself. It's that simple."

Black: Josh, tell me what started you on the path to creating your own law firm.

Hertz: I come from a long line of entrepreneurs, and I saw that they were able to do things their way. My grandfather owned a small furniture business in New York City. He was a character that people wouldn't forget. The biggest hotel chains were his clients.

I never thought much about how he got his clients, but later in life realized his secret. He was a small business owner. He was not the biggest or the cheapest, but he had charisma—that is how he developed business. It was the relationships he built throughout his career. Everyone remembered him because he was so charismatic and memorable. He wore a big cowboy hat and boots, which was quite unusual in New York City.

My father followed a different route. He was a doctor in chemical engineering, but he never gave up his passion of entrepreneurship. Throughout my childhood, he always had his regular nine-to-five job, but also had several side businesses selling chemicals and materials.

My brother—he too was an entrepreneur. He started his law firm straight out of law school back in 1985, which was unheard of back then. He was very charismatic, just like my grandfather. The amazing thing about him starting his law firm right out of law school was the fact that he was in his mid-twenties. He got started by convincing an insurance company to give him all their insurance defense work in the state of Georgia.

I followed in my family's footsteps. Today, I too am an entrepreneur starting my law firm right out of law school.

Black: Give me a little background that led you to your "aha" moment.

Hertz: I had just graduated with a degree in accounting and was working as a plant accountant in South Texas. I spent four grueling years studying accounting and then got a job where I was working nine to five every day, looking at numbers.

Here's the thing—I'm not really a numbers guy. I'm not a person who can sit in a cubicle all day looking at numbers. I got a degree in accounting because I thought it was the right thing to do. But you see, it was not right for me.

My "aha" moment hit me when we were being audited by the IRS. I realized that I really didn't like working as a plant accountant. Not because I was afraid of the challenge, but because I wasn't following my passion. The audit woke me up. I needed to change my life.

I decided to go back to school, packed my bags, and moved to Miami for law school. I loved it, and I saw so many law students fall into the same pattern. The prize was to get a job in a big firm.

Once again, work for another and not for yourself.

As everyone in my school tried tirelessly applying to the big firms, I was working on my business plan of how to start working for myself. After all, I came from a long line of businessmen, and I too would follow my passion. I started my own law firm.

Black: There was a life-changing lesson here, right?

Hertz: Yes. Be a businessperson first, a lawyer second, if you want to thrive in practice and succeed as an entrepreneur. I know this may not be the easiest thing to say, as an attorney, but the bottom line is if you don't bring in business, you cannot be a lawyer working for yourself. It's just that simple.

And this goes back to my point about creating relationships with referral sources, or wherever you get your business. I wanted to be a lawyer, but I wanted to be a businessman first.

I would say if you want to be the best attorney, then work for a large firm where you can devote all your time to lawyering. But if you want to be a businessperson, learn the tricks of the trade and become a relationship builder. I will tell you, clients don't always go to the best and the brightest, but the ones they remember.

Black: What advice would you give other lawyers?

Hertz: Are you a lawyer who is unique in some way? Remember my grandfather, dressed like a cowboy in New York City. Can you make your mark by being different and memorable, just like he did?

Because there are plenty of lawyers out there competing with you and everyone else. Clients do have a choice.

You can be the best attorney in the world, but if you cannot bring in business, you cannot survive. I learned the key to getting referrals was building relationships, just like my grandfather, father, and brother before me.

Black: How did you do it?

Hertz: How did I do it? Networking at bar associations, becoming the leader. You need to realize you can't just join an organization and think referrals are going to drop out of the sky. You must take it to the next level. Become a leader in some capacity. It gives you visibility and credibility. This might take some time, but why join an organization if you're not going to give it your best?

Remember, great is the enemy of good. Be great at networking, not just good. Think outside the box of networking and building relationships.

I started a nonprofit bar association, Dominican-American Bar Association. I was thrust into the spotlight, and got calls every month from prospective clients because of this great exposure. Now, the calls might not be the type of law I practice, but I can refer them out to other lawyers in the nonprofit business. I just essentially built a huge network by starting the nonprofit.

If you see a need in an area and you feel some passion or connection, then that might be a good fit for you. Let's face it, we're not selling widgets; we're selling ability and trust.

Black: So where are you today?

Hertz: Today I work hard every day, but I have peace of mind that I am the businessperson I have always wanted to be; that I'm not working nine to five to put profits into someone else's pocket. Rather, I'm working hard for my family and me.

Throughout the years, I've built many relationships that have helped me to grow and learn every day, because relationships of all kinds matter. They fuel constant growth and are the keys to my success.

I have to say that everyone's path is different and there's no right or wrong way to figure out what works for you.

Black: What do you think was the most important lesson?

Hertz: Always believe in yourself. You can do anything you really put your mind to. It may take several attempts, and the first time, you may fall flat on your face. The point is that you get back up and give it another try and keep moving forward. When you look back on it, sometimes failing turns out to be the best thing that happened to you, but it's hard to believe at that moment.

Black: So tell me, how does all this make you feel?

Hertz: I feel a great sense of accomplishment, including all my failures to where I've got to today. I love what my dad used to tell us: "Success is not final, and failure is not fatal." I later found out that it was a Winston Churchill quote, and there was more: "It is the courage to continue that counts."

I try to live by those words and continue to build relationships that will grow my practice alongside my personal life every single day. I am thankful I took that first step to becoming the businessman, lawyer, husband, father, and entrepreneur I am today.

Joshua points out that at the core of a successful practice is the strength of your relationships, your commitment to leadership, and being a businessperson first.

Believe in yourself. You can do it!

If you fail, get back up and keep moving forward.

And Joshua's words are worth noting: when you look back on it, sometimes failing turns out to be the best thing that happened to you, but it's hard to believe it at the time.

Alex Bokor is a judge with a career path that shows you what can happen when you do life your own way.

Judge Alex Bokor
County Court Judge for the 11th Judicial Circuit of Florida

" *I also felt guilty and a little mad at myself. How could I be unfulfilled when I was doing everything I set out to do?* "

Black: You have had a zigzag career path, and I'm sure there were many times you felt like a fish out of water for even thinking about another way of doing things. Tell me about it.

Bokor: Well, Paula, I really started off on a traditional path that many of my successful friends at big firms followed. I did well in undergrad, excelled at research and writing, volunteered in the local community, and felt like law school was the right path for me.

My hard work was rewarded with admission to the University of Pennsylvania Law School. I was a good student, got good grades, continued to be involved in the community by volunteering at a local inner-city school, and was set on a path of a summer associate position and an offer of employment at Jones Day in New York. By every law school and job metric, I was succeeding.

Once I got to Jones Day, I did interesting work, had mentors who really invested time and effort into my development, and I made some great friends. I was at a job at the top of the legal market. I was doing well, and for the most part, I enjoyed it.

But deep down, even though I was working hard on partnership track and getting all the right feedback, I had this feeling that I was missing something. I tried to bury it, but like Poe's tell-tale heart, it just came back again and again, thumping and thumping in my conscience and subconscious.

Why wasn't I able to visualize becoming partner? Thump.

Why did I feel like I wanted to leave the conversation when the topic was comparing salaries and bonuses and talking about who was up for promotion? Thump.

I knew most associates don't stay with their original firm, or even stay with big law, but I felt a bigger issue.

Black: Did you want to change firms?

Bokor: I didn't want to change firms. I loved my firm. But I just knew I wanted something different. I didn't know what, and that scared me. I certainly didn't want to leave this path without knowing more answers, and all I had were more questions.

And even though I was happy on some level with my successes, I also felt guilty, and a little mad at myself. How could I be unfulfilled when I was doing everything I set out to do?

This really was a case of it's not you, it's me, but I didn't even know what I wanted.

Black: How did you find the courage to buck the system?

Bokor: I was okay with a new challenge, but I just didn't know what I wanted. So I think the first step was simply recognizing that I wanted something else. And the second, maybe more important ingredient, was a little bit of luck at just the right time.

And that luck came from a colleague of mine at Jones Day who was going to clerk for a federal district judge. That's something I'm interested in! But at that time, most judges hired right out of law school, not after two years of practice.

So I went to my colleague's office, and she graciously answered my questions. But here's the lucky part: the judge she was clerking for was looking for a second clerk. So I meekly asked her where, thinking it was going to be in Alaska, but it turns out it was in Tampa, my hometown!

Now all I had to do was get the job and let the firm know that I wanted them to keep my job open for me. Easier said than done. But after an interview, I got the job, and my firm was incredibly gracious. They basically told me, we'll have to make the formal decision after the clerkship, but you're welcome back anytime.

I really was honored to work at such a great place.

Black: You probably had to take a pay cut. How did you deal with that?

Bokor: I was too naive to be concerned with the pay cut, and by the time I realized how big a bite it was, it was too late. I was packing up my bags for Tampa and my clerkship.

So this was my first zigzag. I know, a federal clerkship doesn't exactly sound like a wild adventure, especially with the near-promise of a return ticket to Big Law. But coming from a law school that expected only Big Law employment, Southern District of New York or appeals court clerkships, and maybe Department of Justice jobs, this was at least a step off the path. A step to fulfilling my dreams, and not just following the most comfortable and well-worn path. And I knew this was just the beginning of opening me up to new opportunities.

Black: When you landed the clerkship, what did you love about it, and what did you learn?

Bokor: I loved my clerkship. I had a mentor, Judge Steven D. Merryday, and a feeling like I was really a public servant. I always felt like I was working on important matters at the firm, but now I felt like I was serving the public at large. I loved the feeling and I was humbled by the responsibility. Get it right and you do justice, get it wrong and you cost someone money, time, and in criminal cases, their freedom.

The judge taught me that no matter how smart you think you are, you should always be a humble student of the law, even if you are the one making decisions. This was definitely a different feeling than I got practicing at a big firm.

I now had the taste for public service. I had the idea planted for judicial service in the future. I thought the clerkship would open opportunities, and it did, but what I didn't expect was that the opportunity I wanted was to continue in public service. But I was twenty-six years old or so and I knew I needed more growth, more work, more seasoning, and more time until the right opportunity presented itself.

Black: So what happened next?

Bokor: I was now zigzagging all over the place, from Jones Day, to clerk, back to the big firm, then a boutique firm in Miami—Kozyak Tropin & Throckmorton—but I knew I was growing each step of the way and I was happier and more fulfilled with each move.

But I wanted to combine that career growth with that service bug and that desire was only amplified by working at the firm for slightly over two years and seeing what they do in the community. I wanted to make my mark. And while I was at the firm, I got involved in the local community and had great in-house mentors. Those mentorships and that community involvement connected me with the Miami-Dade County Attorney's Office.

Black: Why was that important?

Bokor: I was prepared to make another zag, but this time I was really going for an opportunity to serve the public at large. An opportunity, I might add, that is not one that the top ten law schools advertise or even really encourage, although they should. But I took that path and I got the opportunity to serve for more than eight years at the Miami-Dade County Attorney's Office—the best public law firm and perhaps the best practicing law job and firm overall, I humbly suggest, in the United States.

Black: How so?

Bokor: I really served the community in so many ways and felt like I was making an impact every day. I worked on litigation and legislative matters, negotiated deals, learned multiple practice areas, and grew as an attorney and public servant. This was the best zigzag so far. But there was one more frontier—judicial service.

I loved serving as an assistant county attorney. I had amazing colleagues with the same commitment, incredible bosses and mentors, and through my leadership and teamwork, I knew I was making my mark on the community.

Black: Was that voice in your heart still speaking to you?

Bokor: My desire to roll up my sleeves and serve the community even more directly was still there. I wanted to take one more leap, one final zig. I wanted to be directly responsible for impacting the community. Not just as a lawyer, not just as an advocate. I wanted some skin in the game. I wanted to chase my ultimate dream of service, so I applied, and three times was nominated by the judicial nominating commission as a county court judge, with Governor Scott selecting me on my third time.

Having to go through the process a few times just made the journey all the sweeter.

Judge Bokor shows us that there is a path to contentment and success, even if it isn't so clear. Sometimes the path just needs to reveal itself one step at a time.

His story illustrates that following the norm may not be for everyone.

And most importantly, he reminds you to never stop listening to your gut.

Chapter Eight

Finding Your Niche: It Takes Courage, Vision, and Tenacity

When I talk to lawyers about finding a niche, there's usually an audible groan.

Most lawyers want to leave their options open. They say, "I can do a lot of things, so why not make a list that says that I can do them all?" Two reasons come to mind.

One is that a long list signals that you're not an expert at any of them. And two, it's hard to get referrals, because no one can remember what you do.

It takes courage and vision to draw a line in the sand and declare your specialty—your little corner of the world, so to speak. And it requires tenacity to become known for that niche, so you need to enjoy it.

Not many lawyers have the courage, the vision, or the tenacity to become known for a specialty like Daniel Benavides, Michelle Estlund, and Antonio Gallegos. They will each tell you how they found a niche they enjoy and became an authority in the area.

Daniel Benavides is a Harvard Law grad that had a rude awakening. It helped him find his niche. He stayed the course, and leveraged it for both his firm and himself.

Daniel Benavides
*Partner at Shutts & Bowen,
where he is a member of the
Real Estate Practice Group*

"*My experiences taught me that law is not a profession, law is a business. Law firms will only keep you around as long as you make them money.*"

Black: Danny, I understand you had a pretty heady beginning. Tell me about it.

Benavides: Ever since I can remember, my father pushed me to go to Harvard Law School. I never expected that I would actually get into Harvard Law, but when I did, I really had no choice but to go.

I started law school in 2004 at the height of the boom before the Great Recession. Top law firms literally begged to hire us. They offered us $200,000-a-year starting salaries plus signing bonuses. They courted us with ridiculously lavish summer programs—that included nightly spending stipends, all-expenses-paid trips to Vegas, and Hummer-sines to chauffeur us anywhere we wanted.

Black: So with all that courting, where did you decide to go?

Benavides: I ultimately chose to work at Fried Frank in New York. I wanted to do real estate, and they were widely considered the number one real estate firm in the United States. The head of the real estate department, and perhaps the top real estate attorney in New York, became a close personal friend and mentor while I was in law school.

Fried Frank did not disappoint. I was put on some of the most high-profile real estate deals in the United States. As a mere first year, I was working closely with legendary real estate moguls and closing multibillion-dollar transactions. I was on top of the world. I thought I was untouchable.

Black: I understand you had a rude awakening. Do you want to tell me about it?

Benavides: Then my world, along with the global economy, came crashing down. Until 2008, most "experts" believed the real estate market would plateau, or perhaps at worst decline slightly. But by 2008, it became clear that they were terribly wrong. Real estate deals suddenly came to a screeching halt.

For about three months, I sat at my desk with nothing to do but contemplate my reality. I figured it was only a matter of time before I got laid off. There was no way my firm would keep a cocky and inexperienced second-year associate around, when even senior associates and partners had nothing to do.

Black: What did you do during that time?

Benavides: I started looking around for other jobs, but no one was hiring young attorneys without any experience or any portable book of business. After months of a nationwide search, I was fortunate to find an opening at a boutique bankruptcy and commercial litigation firm in Miami, Florida. The job paid a lot less than I was making in New York, but at least the work was interesting and the people were incredible.

Most of my former colleagues at Fried Frank and at other law firms in New York, who began their search later than I did, were not so lucky. Many were laid off, and had to move back in with their parents while they looked for work. Some stopped practicing law altogether. These are Ivy League graduates working at top real estate firms that could not find a job. I was lucky.

Black: What did this experience teach you?

Benavides: My experiences taught me that law is not a profession. Law is a business. Law firms will only keep you around as long as you make them money, period. They don't care that you have a J.D. or even a Harvard J.D. They don't care how smart you are, or how smart you think you are. All that matters at the end of the day is the bottom line. If you make them more money than you cost them, you stay. Otherwise, you go—it's that simple.

I also learned that today's legal profession is highly competitive. There are staggering numbers of smart and experienced lawyers out there willing to take your place for less money. There are so many lawyers that we have effectively become fungible commodities.

We're no longer professionals with the luxury of sitting behind a desk waiting for a phone to ring. As technology continues to advance, it's only a matter of time before many tasks done by attorneys today, especially young attorneys, become completely obsolete.

Black: How did this knowledge change your course?

Benavides: If you want to survive in this business, you have to learn to adapt. For my part, I identified a great niche in hospitality. I realized that most attorneys who call themselves hospitality attorneys are actually practitioners in other areas, such as real estate, land use, or employment law, who sometimes assist hospitality clients, along with clients in other industries—and that's fine.

But almost none of them dedicate their practice exclusively to the hospitality industry and the unique issues that face that industry, which means that those lawyers are not as experienced and efficient at handling those issues as somebody who does that every day. And more importantly, they don't market themselves that way.

Black: So how did you leverage that?

Benavides: This unique marketing twist allowed me to be where clients are instead of where attorneys are. For example, I am a member of several hospitality industry organizations that most attorneys have never even heard of, much less thought to network there, but many potential clients are members of those organizations. And being the only lawyer in the room has serious advantages.

Black: So what were the results the strategy produced?

Benavides: Over the last two years, my book of business has quadrupled and my presence in the local hospitality industry has become ubiquitous, thanks in large part to being a member of those organizations.

I've also been involved with some of the most important hospitality-related matters of the last decade. Some of my cases are discussed at industry conferences and in industry publications nationwide.

Black: What does your practice look like today?

Benavides: I represent hotels, restaurants, and nightclubs, sort of as an outside general counsel. I delegate a lot of hourly billable work to my partners and sometimes get the firm some good press. I bring in sufficient steady business to justify my existence to my law firm.

This allows me to take the pressure off of my billable hours, and as an added bonus for someone who loves to travel and eat, I get to network where I play. I couldn't be happier.

Black: Do you have advice for younger attorneys?

Benavides: My advice to younger attorneys who plan to stay in private practice for the next few decades is to dedicate a substantial amount of time and effort to bringing in business. You can do that in many ways. You can become an expert in an industry or in a new hot area of law. Network, write, and market yourself constantly, both inside and outside your firm. Think outside the box, and be where other attorneys have not yet arrived.

Help or mentor other attorneys. You never know—they may one day return the favor.

Always be mindful of your reputation as an ethical, hard-working attorney. Advocate for your clients. Be responsible, and deliver quality work timely and efficiently.

Be willing to negotiate bills. And, most importantly, always make clients feel like they got what they paid for.

Make no mistake, developing and maintaining a book of business is hard work. You will be working most weekends, and you can toss your nine a.m. to six p.m. workday dreams out the window. Your vacations will be interrupted constantly.

It's certainly easier and more comfortable to sit behind a desk and wait for a partner to come in with the next big billable assignment, but nothing good comes easy.

Black: No, it doesn't.

Danny Benavides's story reminds us how important it is to be honest with yourself and have a sense of what is happening around you. He was able to see the writing on the wall so he could do something about it before the market was flooded with unemployed lawyers.

Being an indispensable adviser that understands many aspects of a client's business grows the relationship. Danny does that so well. And, most importantly, he likes the hospitality industry.

I love what he said about the fact that building a book of business will be hard—because it will be! But that doesn't mean you can't have fun if you pick an area you like, and do it with people you like. And that, my friends, will add to the enjoyment of doing it.

I can attest to that from my own experience. I love working with smart, ambitious lawyers. It was one of the best decisions I made to focus on the legal profession. I built a life I love.

So think about it—would you rather sit back and wait for others to feed you or would you like to be growing a practice you love? Find a niche and become an expert.

Michelle Estlund found her niche. She is the most recognized Interpol defense lawyer in the world. Yes, I said *world*.

Michelle Estlund
Criminal defense attorney and preeminent Interpol defense lawyer

I eventually accepted that no one knows everything, even experts."

Black: Michelle, what was going on with your practice when you realized something needed to change?

Estlund: I had been practicing criminal defense for most of my career when I met you, and I really enjoyed it, but I was also feeling complacent. I knew that I wanted to add something to my practice and grow it into a very complementary part of my life, rather than just have a job or even just a career.

And I remember that in our discussions you had told me several times about developing a niche practice and to kind of be on the lookout for that. I remember you encouraged me to focus on a very specific area. And I had heard this from other sources also, but it seemed like so many things related to criminal law were already saturated with specialty attorneys.

I knew that I loved criminal law. I loved human rights and politics. But I didn't really honestly think I could mesh all those things together in a law practice that I both cared about and would be lucrative. I thought, That will just never happen.

Black: Explain how your "aha" moment came about.

Estlund: I remember that a client walked into my office with an Interpol case and asked if I could help. This client was wanted out of Venezuela. This was at a time when the Venezuelan government was nationalizing various industries—including the banking industry. And in order to obtain the assets being held by this particular bank, the government had issued arrest warrants for the heads of the bank and the people who were on the board of directors, including that particular client.

I started researching extensively, and what I realized was that there was no real in-depth treatment of Interpol anywhere online. I saw that even the attorneys who were advertising themselves as being experienced were in fact not, once you did a little bit of digging. Nobody was looking at this on a profound level and I realized I could do better than nobody.

Black: I remember what happened next.

Estlund: I told you, "I think I have an idea," and I told you about the Interpol research I had done and the client that had approached me. And I remember you smiled and told me I had to give you my credit card so we could buy a URL and start a blog. I remember that I did take out my credit card and hand it to you, and I did not want to let go of it because I knew that once I did, that this thing was going to start—and that was really scary for me.

I remember that you told me, "You'll be the leading expert on Interpol," and I knew that you were a crazy person. And turns out that kind of ended up happening, didn't it?

Black: What were the obstacles that almost stopped you?

Estlund: I think my primary limitation at that time was a concern or a fear of criticism. And this might sound odd coming from somebody who is a criminal defense trial attorney, who should be used to criticism and used to hearing no, but this was different for me, because it wasn't a set of facts in a case that was presented to me, for me to protect and defend another person. This was for me, which is often more difficult. It was my writing, my thoughts, and my ideas. The idea of something that personal being critiqued was very challenging for me.

I wanted to start a blog that was geared toward other attorneys, potential clients, academics, and people like that with the goal of educating people about Interpol, establishing credibility for myself, I wanted to attract clients, of course, and I wanted to advocate for reform where it was needed. Like I said, part of what I wanted to do was advocate for reform of Interpol proceedings, and I was worried that people would think, well, who does she think she is? Why would we listen to this Miami lawyer over in Europe?

This is an international, quasi-legal organization, and I just didn't feel that I had the gravitas that I needed in order to effect change.

Also, I was worried more personally for my practice—that if I publicized myself as being a specialist or focusing in a niche practice, people would think that that's all I could do, that I'm a one-trick pony. So those were my concerns.

Black: What was your strategy?

Estlund: In terms of strategy, I can't say that I had a specific strategy thought out, other than I knew who my target audience was going to be, and I knew that I wanted to serve as a source of information that wasn't otherwise readily available. And I hoped that consistent blogging about my topic would also force me to stay on my toes, and it has.

Black: So what did you learn, and how did you muster up the courage?

Estlund: I eventually accepted that no one knows everything, even experts. And I remembered my favorite, most well respected professors and mentors throughout my life all had something in common. It was that they didn't back away from saying "I don't know," because they loved what they did, and they knew how to go find out the information that they needed. I knew I could do that too.

I also realized that we can't wait until we're not afraid to act. It's not brave if you're not scared. Even the most seasoned attorneys are afraid of something. For me, it's not judges, it's not juries, it's not law enforcement officers, and it's not public speaking. For me, what I was really afraid of was writing about something I cared about and having it not be perfect in public and online.

I worked obsessively for weeks to research, write, and edit my first few posts that would be used to launch my blog. I liked what I wrote, but then I almost didn't publish, because everything would be out there, and that was really scary for me.

There is a movie called *We Bought a Zoo,* and there's a line in that movie that goes like this: the lead character says, "You know, sometimes all you need is twenty seconds of insane courage, just literally twenty seconds of just embarrassing bravery, and I promise you something great will come of it."

For me, simple and small as it sounds, my twenty seconds were when I clicked *publish* and nothing bad happened. Actually, nothing happened at all for two or three months, and then my readership went up. The Department of Justice and Interpol and universities and private individuals were reading my blog, and I knew it because I could see my analytics. People started calling me. People started consulting me. And people started retaining me.

Black: What do you find satisfying about your practice now?

Estlund: I have to say that one of the most satisfying elements of my practice is that I can provide my clients with one of the most basic human needs, and that is to be heard. When they tell me their stories, and I put the story into writing, and I back it up with evidence, we submit that to Interpol and ask for help.

Many of my clients have expressed to me that even after our first meeting they feel a sense of relief and release just from being heard. And by the time we bring their case to the attention of Interpol, they know that someone has not only listened, but is on their side in a pretty epic battle. That is extremely valuable to me on a personal level.

Black: What advice would you give others?

Estlund: I guess I would first say, you need to invest financially and invest your time in your craft, if you want to be outstanding. Nobody wants to spend money on un-fun stuff. When you spend money in targeted ways, to advance your career, it does come back to you.

I travel to seminars, even if I'm not speaking or even if they're very small, when I know that someone I want to meet will be there, or that I will learn something, even if it's little. Most people won't do that.

I spend money on my blog maintenance—although you can do them for free, too—because I get better traction that way and that traction brings me cases.

I take time, aside from actually working on my cases, to write a blog, to maintain contact with people who are in the field, and to stay on top of my game, because I know that if I don't, somebody else will.

When you're in doubt about doing something or not, do the affirmative. Say yes. Just do it. If you take a step, or if you say yes to an opportunity, something could happen. It's not certain, but if you don't take the step, nothing will happen—and that is certain.

Listen, it can be easy to burn out. It can be really easy to lose steam or lose faith. The law is hard work when it's done right. But when you seek out motivated people, or you go to relevant seminars, or you reach out to congratulate someone, or just ask a colleague to lunch to learn more about how they work at a personal or professional level, you're increasing your level of engagement in your profession.

The law is personal, or at least it should be, in my opinion. Staying engaged allows us to stay motivated, relevant, and informed. And that's how our practices can feel more alive and more vibrant.

Black: What does your Interpol practice look like today?

Estlund: I've been really, really lucky after including Interpol in my practice to be able to see that both domestic and international government agencies read my blog, that leading human rights organizations in the United States and Europe consult with me on Interpol issues.

I even was able to attend a European parliament symposium on red-notice abuse. Not a lot of people have had a chance to do that, and that's what this has done for my practice.

I have clients from all over the globe that I've successfully represented before Interpol, and I talk with journalists on Interpol matters pretty frequently, and give interviews to the media and advise about Interpol matters.

I've developed new contacts with attorneys who live abroad, and I have friendships that I never would have anticipated. I think that one of the best things that's come about as a result of my Interpol practice is that I had the privilege of representing a former CIA operative pro bono in a case where the US government, in my opinion, abandoned him.

My blog readership now includes people from all over the world—think tanks, journalists, academics, prospective and past clients, and other attorneys. I've seen that my practice has evolved. I now am able to be more selective in the number and the types of cases that I choose to accept. And my fee structure has evolved as well.

Black: Are you glad you gave me your credit card that day years ago?

Estlund: I am. I thought you were so crazy, but yes. Yes.

Michelle's story illustrates the power of drawing a line in the sand. She found a niche that she was passionate about on multiple levels, made a commitment, even though it was scary, and she never looked back.

Michelle set out to invest her time and money to differentiate herself in her local market. What she found was a global community she loves working with and clients she connects to on a profound level. She created a life, not just a living.

Antonio Gallegos found his niche in FDA and compliance matters, which led him to become senior corporate counsel in his chosen industry. He was tenacious and focused all along the way.

Antonio Gallegos
*Senior Corporate Counsel,
Leprino Foods, and formerly
Of Counsel at Greenberg
Traurig*

In this three-way battle for time, workload and family often won, leaving business development to the side."

Black: Talk about your big firm experience and struggles to cultivate your own clients and how you didn't just passively wait to be fed.

Gallegos: I worked at three large firms from 2000 to 2017. Business development was always stressed, but I didn't receive much support from the firm for the first five years or so. I was basically told, "Go hunt, but don't let your billable hours fall." It was often difficult to balance my billable workload with the networking I needed to do to develop my own practice.

I always made family a top priority.

I have a wife of seventeen years and two teenage boys, so in this three-way battle for my time, workload and family often won, leaving business development to the side. But this allowed me to develop a high level of experience in two practice areas, which are the foundation for me to build my own practice—FDA regulations and products liability litigation.

Black: What was your strategy to find a niche that you would like and a place where you could become known?

Gallegos: Well, about six years into my career, it became apparent that I needed to market myself in a specific niche if I was going to build my own practice. So I asked myself, what is my passion for my personal life that I can incorporate into my legal career?

Well, I was a professional cyclist for three years, still an avid competitive cyclist at the amateur level, and I loved the outdoors. So I chose sports, anti-doping and Olympic-related disputes.

I really loved this work, and the networking was a lot of fun. I built name recognition by writing articles for cycling magazines, and I received lots of calls and inquiries from athletes as potential clients, but only a select few could pay big-firm rates. And even when I discounted my fees, it often wasn't enough.

I was the only lawyer at my firm doing any work in sports, so support from the top was kind of lukewarm. They really liked my passion, but less-than-stellar financial results and not contributing to another practice group made things a little difficult.

I decided to build a niche more closely aligned to my FDA and products liability experience, representing companies in the food and nutrition industries. This fit well with my interest in sports and healthy living. I also had some work experience in this area prior to law school—working for a media and trade show company that focused on the natural products industry.

I began writing articles on food and nutrition regulations, reconnecting with industry contacts, and marketing myself internally at the law firm. No one else worked on food-specific legal issues, but plenty of others advised food companies in other areas of law, like corporate-led employment work.

I eventually changed law firms to join an established food law practice group. Having that support was great, but I needed to distinguish myself from other lawyers in the group. I decided to leverage my language skills and ethnic background to focus on the Hispanic and Latino food industries. US companies had focused on this population, and foreign companies tried to enter the US market.

Black: Antonio, you have become a master at working trade shows. Talk about your methodology before the conference, at the conference, and, most importantly, follow-up after the conference.

Gallegos: I look for food and nutrition industry events, where potential clients would be—trade shows, business seminars, and things like that.

Bar association events, even those that were focused on my niche, were never a priority. Networking with lawyers is good for getting referrals, but doesn't allow for direct connection with the potential client. Even when I'd get a referral from time to time, that attorney was often very protective of his or her relationship with the client.

For conferences, I always reviewed the attendee list in advance to identify my top prospects. Then I researched those companies so I could be prepared to talk about their business in a way that highlights my experience, but I always made sure the emphasis was on their business.

When talking with prospects, I also looked for clues into their personal interests and hobbies, and looked for common ground. For me, it was things like sports, the outdoors, travel, and family. I would talk with as many people as possible, but always make sure to make at least five meaningful personal connections.

I was always hunting for speaking engagements. I would send articles I had written on timely legal issues for the food and nutrition industry to the trade show and seminar organizers, and offer to present on those topics. Speaking engagements are a good way for potential clients to see you as an authority. You know the people who attend are interested, so it's relatively easy to get them to approach you, just by taking questions during the presentation or inviting them to stay afterwards for more discussion.

For follow-up, I would always send emails approximately a week or so after the conference. And not generic canned greetings, but messages that had specific topics from our discussions we had had. And I'd try to include a personal note about common non-business interests. Then I'd find a way to reconnect every month, sending them my newsletter, forwarding an article or legal notice relevant to their business.

Black: Antonio, that is masterful. What were your goals?

Gallegos: The primary goal was building a reputation as a go-to lawyer in my niche. First it was sports, then food and nutrition, and then, more specifically, the Latin and Hispanic food and nutrition industries.

Most people I talked to at trade shows didn't need to hire me right away, but by reaching out to them at their industry events and staying in regular communication, I hoped to be the one they'd think of first when they needed help on food-related legal issues. As I built this network, I wanted people in this industry to feel that I knew their business and that we had connected on a personal level.

Black: Going in-house wasn't the ultimate goal, was it?

Gallegos: Networking in the food industry and regular communication with my contacts is how I ended up in-house. I had reached out to the assistant general counsel several years before moving to the company, trying to get their legal work. I added him to my newsletter email list and sent him emails periodically to keep in touch. In one of these follow-ups, he mentioned that he had just lost one of their longtime in-house lawyers.

I wasn't looking to make any moves at the time. My efforts in the Latino and Hispanic food markets were starting to show some real promise, but I'm always willing to consider my options. And because I had a solid foundation in my law firm, I was able to take the time and make sure this in-house position was truly a great opportunity for me.

I used my breadth of experience to convince him to modify the job duties to a position that gave me better opportunities to advance myself inside the company. So in May of 2017, I was hired as senior corporate counsel for a Denver-based food company, and they're the world's largest producer of mozzarella cheese and an industry leader in other dairy products, like whey protein for nutrition products and lactose for infant formulas.

Black: What is it like working in-house? How do you see your previous experience as a foundation for what you're doing today?

Gallegos: Working inside the company, understanding how business works, and the risk tolerance of senior leadership is critical. The approach I took to business development and serving clients in private practice was a good foundation for this. And that's basically listening to people talk about their business and their concerns. Working in-house, expectations to know the business objectives are even higher, but luckily, being on the inside makes it a little easier to gain these insights.

Black: What advice would you give others?

Gallegos: First, make sure your legal skills are solid. People know when you're faking it. But at the same time, understand that the law is not your client's primary concern, and they're really not interested in what the law actually says. They want to know what their companies can and cannot do to meet business objectives. They want to know where the gray areas are, and whether their business plans keep them sufficiently inside of the gray, or whether they're pushing too close to the edge.

Get to know what makes your clients tick and how they fit into their respective markets relative to their competitors. Look for opportunities to meet your clients at their offices to get a glimpse of what their world looks like. You'll be surprised at how favorably your clients react when you incorporate seemingly small observations about their businesses and their competitor behaviors into your legal advice.

Antonio Gallegos understood what it takes to make a name for himself in a niche area.

First he found something he was passionate about. That helped him keep his enthusiasm. Then he wrote articles and a newsletter to demonstrate his expertise. He found speaking gigs to get in front of his potential clients and start to form a bond. And most importantly, he did it all with the focus and sensitivity to what his clients want and need.

Antonio is truly a master at working trade shows and conferences. I would suggest that you read his methodology over again and take meticulous notes—he's Obi-Wan Kenobi.

Chapter Nine

Job Security
Is a Myth

Job security is a myth.

Okay, certainly a judicial lifetime appointment is job security, but nowhere else in the legal profession is there a lifetime appointment. You are subject to the economy, governmental politics, internal politics, management decisions, and the list goes on. That's the reality.

So how can you hedge your bet, so to speak? Create a safety net that will be there when you need it, because no job, no client, no position lasts forever.

How do you create a safety net? You need a personal brand.

What differentiates you from the six million other lawyers on the planet? How are you being perceived? How do you want to be perceived?

What do people know about you? Do your colleagues and potential clients or employers know what you do and how you do it? Do your friends and family know? Do they know what you're committed to, what you're passionate about and what lights your fire? Do you have a niche they can understand and remember?

Probably not. They may know things about you, but it's not a story you crafted with intention and strategy. If you're employed, you need to think about your personal brand, your reputation, your strengths, and how they are communicated to the outside world.

Equally as important is how you communicate them within your organization. How do you want your colleagues to perceive you? If you're a solo or small firm, it is imperative that the outside world knows and understands your brand. Give them a reason to choose you to handle their matter.

Clients come and go. Job situations change. Create your safety net: your brand. It's communicated by what you do and how you do it. And you can use internet marketing techniques to amplify it.

Marc Cerniglia and Daniel Decker are legal marketing experts who will give you an interesting perspective that could be a game changer.

Legal marketing strategist Marc Cerniglia sheds lights on what your marketing focus should be, and I think you will be a bit surprised.

Marc Cerniglia
Founding partner of Spotlight Branding; helps lawyers navigate the truths and myths about internet marketing

"The issue is . . . the strategies that get sacrificed and neglected because this point of view creates tunnel vision for lawyers."

Black: Marc, I know you're on a mission when it comes to law firm marketing. Tell me a little bit about it.

Cerniglia: I'm on a mission to debunk the illusion that most internet marketing companies perpetuate. They preach the gospel of SEO—search-engine optimization—and where you show up on Google, as if that's all that matters when it comes to the internet.

You know, it's so unfortunate how that message has really taken over. And many lawyers and most industries—if we're being honest—are bowing down at the altar of SEO, whether they know it or not. You know, I know that might sound kind of intense, but I think it's a message that has really permeated the way most people think about internet marketing.

I think if we don't step back and actually think critically about that approach—the focus on search engines—it becomes too easy to just become a lemming that follows the rest of the pack into believing this SEO gospel as truth.

You know—and here's the real interesting thing—the issue with this isn't just the potential wasted money, time, and energy by investing in an SEO campaign. It's missing what else the internet can do for your law firm. It's the strategies that get sacrificed and neglected because this point of view creates tunnel vision for lawyers.

Black: So it sort of lets lawyers off the hook. It's a quick fix, and the lawyers can get back to lawyering. Okay then, what strategies are being neglected?

Cerniglia: So this is actually where it's so interesting to me. What I see is that the strategies that are being neglected are actually marketing principles that have been true for as long as we know and have specifically worked well for law firms—things such as the importance of staying top-of-mind;

staying connected with people, which generates more referrals; or the importance of building a strong brand, which is just a marketing buzzword for your reputation, your credibility, what people think about your firm. That's your brand. And then, you know, top-of-mind awareness, building a strong brand as a credible expert.

These are tried and true marketing principles that have stood the test of time. Yet, when it comes to the internet, these strategies are rarely discussed.

Black: Well, let's talk about that for a minute. Why do you suggest that it's not a good idea to focus on SEO?

Cerniglia: Well, there are really two sides to it. First, the fact that I think it takes away from focusing on other strategies, which is what we really discussed a little bit so far. But second, and to it put it simply, I think the success rate is just minimal when it comes to SEO, and I think it's only going to get worse.

I mean, if you stop and think about it, search engines literally have limited prime real estate. I mean, if you're on the fifth page, you might as well be on the fiftieth. Everyone knows that what really matters is getting on page one, and of course, if possible, getting to the top. So let's talk about that a bit more.

I mean, how many websites can rank on the first page, about ten or so? Only ten! Out of how many law firms in your area that do what you do? Probably hundreds. And then, of course, how many can be number one? Literally only one. There's only one spot. It's like a ton of people all paying for the same billboard, but only one law firm actually showing up on the billboard—that would be foolish.

Now, don't get me wrong. I mean, somebody gets to be number one, and that could be anyone. I'm not saying SEO is wrong, nor am I saying you have to ignore it. What I am saying is that oftentimes I think it's simply just not worth it. And I don't think it's where the focus needs to be.

Not only is it a tough road, but there's so much more the internet can do for a law practice, and I really like seeing the focus shift toward those things.

And it's only going to get more difficult, I think, as more and more people open up firms, build a website, and hire SEO companies. I mean, how many companies don't offer an SEO package in one of their basic website plans? Well, actually, I know one. I happen to own it.

Black: Of course. You have firsthand experience with helping law firms shift their focus when it comes to marketing. So what are some of the specific strategies you've seen work well?

Cerniglia: You know, I think this might be one of the most surprising things of everything we've talked about. There isn't really anything new or innovative that needs to be done.

Websites, blogging, email newsletters, social media—these are the foundations of the internet. I think it's about shifting the thinking, and how lawyers execute these things so that they focus on the right strategies. In other words, the tools don't need to change, but how they're used does.

You and I have actually talked about this before, right? I mean, a hammer is a tool. I can use a hammer to hang a picture or build a house. Same tool, two very different outcomes and different methods of using the tool to get there.

So it's like this: all of a sudden, blogging isn't about Google and keywords. It's about creating content that educates an audience and provides practical advice. Social media isn't about whether or not you can get new clients through Facebook, and instead it's about what the rest of humanity uses it for, which is to stay in touch with people. I mean, staying top-of-mind, that's the purpose of social media.

And I don't think that's it. I think things like sending an email newsletter become as obvious as having a business card. If you don't have that regular touch point, you're missing out on referrals. And then of course, Paula, there's your website. Your website is a brochure. It's meant to showcase what you do and move people forward in wanting to work with you or refer to you.

I think content becomes simpler, more condensed and to the point, rather than being long-winded, so Google will like the length and the keywords. I think websites become clean and easy to navigate, rather than cluttered and busy.

And then finally, I think that over atop all of this is a focus on the brand, on your story, finding ways to communicate to people what you're about, why you care about what you do, and what it is that you do. What are you an expert at? So again, branding, referrals—these strategies have always worked.

Black: Gosh, that's so true. When a lawyer stops thinking about what the Google robots want and thinks about what your actual human audience wants, you begin to see things differently. So Marc, what happens when they begin to focus on these strategies?

Cerniglia: It's been really rewarding, but it can also be challenging at times. These strategies don't work overnight. And I think there are some misconceptions out there that are actually probably worth clearing up.

This isn't the kind of marketing where you can just set it and forget it. You have to continue to grow your audience. For example, your email newsletter is only as powerful as the size of your email list, but there are so many places to get emails, right? Networking, clients, colleagues, heck, every phone call that comes in, you should capture an e-mail address. You've also got to put yourself out there—network, speak, write a book. These are things that experts do.

I think looking in the right places for results is important also. For example, there is a study that says lawyers are only getting about one-third of the referrals they should be getting from people they already know. That right there is enough reason to take our entire conversation seriously. I mean, who cares about getting clients from Google, if there are that many referrals being left on the table? So tracking referrals is definitely one of the most important things.

And then finally—and this is one of my favorite things to share—when you build a brand as one of the best at what you do, you can charge like it. It doesn't mean you're price-gouging people, but if you're one of the best at what you do, and you market yourself appropriately, there is nothing wrong with charging the proper amount. I mean, if you're good, people are going to get what they paid for.

Think about this: Google could destroy your search-engine ranking overnight, but they can never destroy your brand.

Wow, that is pretty eye-opening. Google can change its algorithms, and thus your search-engine rankings, overnight. Do you really want to hand over that kind of control?

Many lawyers buy into the SEO philosophy, because it takes the marketing off their plate—it's the easy way out. There is a place for SEO in your marketing strategy, but making it your sole focus is not a wise decision.

Take Marc's advice. Don't neglect the tried and true marketing principles to stay top-of-mind with your referral sources and prospective clients. When you invest time and energy into those things, you are in control of your brand. Know that there will be a next crossroads and prepare for it. Have a foundation in place.

Legal marketing content and messaging expert Daniel Decker is always looking for better ways to help you communicate with your clients and referral sources. I think you will find his new perspective fascinating.

Daniel Decker
Founding partner of Spotlight Branding; helps lawyers stand out from the crowd

"The challenge for lawyers is: (1) how do I stand out in a sea of competition, and (2) how can I create trust with clients and win new business?"

Black: Daniel, you have a unique way of looking at legal business development. Tell me how it came about.

Decker: So let's start by acknowledging the challenges that lawyers face. Let's be honest—it's hard for lawyers to stand out in a competitive market. We've been working with lawyers for about seven years now and even in that short amount of time, the market has gotten noticeably more crowded.

I think the biggest change in that time span has been the growth of do-it-yourself legal sites, like LegalZoom and Rocket Lawyer. We're also seeing companies like Avvo roll out platforms that are basically like Uber for legal services, where a consumer can pay forty dollars for fifteen minutes on the phone with a lawyer. Meanwhile, law schools are still pumping out forty to fifty thousand graduates pretty much every single year. So it's a competitive space and it's only getting tougher to stand out. So that's challenge number one, if you will.

Number two is that the legal profession has kind of been stigmatized in pop culture and in the media. Lawyers face what I call a "trust deficit" when it comes to bringing in new business. Prospective clients are preconditioned not to trust them or to be skeptical of their motivations.

This isn't just theoretical. The ABA did a study a few years back, which found that an outrageous 69 percent of consumers surveyed believe that lawyers are more interested in making money than in serving their clients. So that obviously creates a roadblock for lawyers looking to grow their business.

So in a nutshell, the challenge for lawyers is: (1) how do I stand out in a sea of competition, and (2) how can I create trust with clients and win new business?

Black: That makes sense. So how do you approach those challenges?

Decker: I want to present a new prism for lawyers to think about their marketing and business development. Their marketing needs to be less about the dry details of describing the practice area and, instead, focus on telling a powerful and compelling story—a story that simplifies their message and makes it easily digestible for their target clients, a story that makes it easy to understand what the lawyer does and how he or she helps people.

I've done a lot of research on this recently, and it's fascinating. Studies show that the human brain can actually process and store information much more effectively when it's presented in a universally recognized story format, probably because, for tens of thousands of years, that's how we've transmitted information from generation to generation.

Black: So tell me about this story. Are there guidelines that lawyers should follow?

Decker: Yes. And before I dive in, remember that I'm not talking about creating a literal storybook. This is a prism, and a guide, that lawyers can use as they develop their business development strategy and build their brand.

Every good story includes four basic elements: there's a hero, the hero has a problem, there's a villain, and there's a trusted guide.

First, the hero. Surprise! The lawyer can't be the hero of his or her own story. This is a shift from conventional thinking. The story isn't about them—it's about their clients. Their clients are the hero of the story.

Second, the hero's problem. The hero has a problem—her husband wants a divorce, his son was charged with a crime, their house is being threatened by the IRS, his business is facing a lawsuit. The hero has a problem.

Third, there's a villain out there, actively making the problem worse and keeping the hero from living a better life. This depends on the lawyer's area of practice, but if the lawyer does tax law, the villain could be the IRS. For a criminal defense lawyer, the villain could be the overly aggressive prosecutors or an unfair justice system in general. For a divorce attorney, the villain could easily become the greedy spouse on the other side of the table. Bottom line, there's a villain out there making life worse for the hero and keeping them from solving their problem.

And finally, there's a trusted guide—think Yoda, Gandalf, or Mr. Miyagi. This is the person with the wisdom, knowledge, experience, and perspective to help the hero understand what's happening to them, to defeat the villain, overcome their problem, and achieve their better life. This is the lawyer's role in the story.

Black: Got it. There's a hero, the hero has a problem, there's a villain, and the lawyer's role is to serve as the trusted guide.

Decker: So if I were talking to a lawyer right now, I would tell them, you need to take some time and think this through. Work on defining each element in your story. Who is the hero? What is their problem? Who or what is the villain? And, finally, most importantly, you have to position yourself as the trusted guide.

Black: Can you give me an example?

Decker: Yes, absolutely. We worked with a lawyer who focuses exclusively on representing high-net-worth women in divorce. That's her hero—those women.

In this story, the problem the hero is facing is that the husband wants a divorce, and she, the hero, is unprepared for life without a spouse. She often has kids and hasn't worked in a decade or more. She's lost, scared, and not sure how to move forward.

Now, the villain in this story is the husband, who is out to fight for every last penny in the settlement, and is willing to do whatever it takes to win.

And the lawyer positions herself as the guide, here to help the hero save the day. She's highly empathetic to her hero, and she understands the fear and uncertainty that these women are experiencing. She's devoted her entire practice to helping these women defeat their villain and create a stable, financially secure new life after divorce.

This lawyer tells her story very, very effectively, and she's been very successful as a result.

So there are two important lessons that I want to point out from this example. The first is that the more the lawyer can narrow their focus and zero in on a niche, the more powerful their story becomes. If they can focus their practice on a single practice area or at least a small group of related practice areas, they're going to tell a much more powerful story, just like so many of your clients.

The second is that the lawyer's main job, after they've defined each character in their story, is to live out their role as the trusted guide. That's who they need to become, day in and day out—the way they answer the phone, the way they listen, the way they interact, even the way they lay out their office.

Black: So how does a lawyer begin to live out that role?

Decker: So they need to focus on two things: establishing empathy and building authority. Empathy just means that they get it—that they understand the pain, the frustration, the fear that the hero is experiencing. And authority means positioning the lawyer as knowledgeable, experienced, and highly qualified to solve the problem and defeat the villain.

Those two things need to be the main focus of the lawyer's business development process and the brand that they're building. Empathy and authority—that allows the attorney to connect in a powerful way with the hero of their story, and it sets the stage for the lawyer to become the trusted guide.

Black: Okay, that makes sense. But let's get practical. How does a lawyer begin?

Decker: A lawyer's marketing, from the first contact with a prospective client all the way to the last, should reflect this story. Now, that often starts with their website. Does it express empathy? Does it establish the attorney as an authority?

This can be hard for lawyers, but the best way for them to establish empathy is by speaking directly to their audience in language that resonates with them. That means drop the legalese. It means acknowledging the emotion they're going through. And it means addressing the fear or the opportunity that they're grappling with.

And then, they can establish authority by demonstrating their expertise. I think that every lawyer should position their website as an educational resource, packed with blog entries, educational video, special reports, white papers, and so forth. When their goal becomes educating prospective clients rather than simply listing off their credentials, they establish their own credibility and authority in the process. We talk about creating an "ACE" brand—authoritative credible expert.

If they're really feeling ambitious, here are two more ideas to establish authority. Number one, write a book. Paula, you've experienced this firsthand. A book is incredibly powerful as a credibility tool, and it won't be as difficult as many people think it is to actually get it done.

And number two, launch a podcast. Podcasts are a very effective business development channel in this day in age, and again, it is not as difficult as you might think to execute.

Black: So Daniel, what's the bottom line?

Decker: So the bottom line for me is that we're operating in a competitive environment and it's only going to get tougher. To really build a sustainable, profitable law practice, lawyers need to learn how to tell a story with their marketing. They need to speak directly to their hero to show him or her how they're going to help them solve their problem, defeat their villain, and get to a better place in life.

And they need to embrace their role as the trusted guide in this journey—their Yoda, their Gandalf, their Mr. Miyagi.

Of course, storytelling has been at the core of our civilization. We relate to stories; it's in our DNA. The biggest point here is that the story isn't about you. That's the real paradigm shift.

So think about how to create a practice area description, résumé, new-client pitch, or website using Daniel's method. It will make a world of difference. Besides, why should you sound like everyone else that does what you do?

Tell a story by any means possible that will demonstrate your difference.

Chapter Ten

Work-Life Balance?

Who came up with that phrase *work-life balance* anyway?

I would like to inform them that we only have one life (that we can verify). Our life is our work and our family and our friends and our hobbies and our errands, etc., etc., etc. It's all our life, and we need to integrate it all, and not to feel guilty about whatever it is we are doing or not doing.

Let's start a movement—my life is a success movement—and rejoice in the successes of each day, from helping to get your children off to school to getting your client off with a lesser charge.

Here's what the bumper stickers will say: Take pride in everything you do, and recognize that not everyone can do what you do. Get help. Yes, hire people to do what you can't do, what you don't want to do, and don't have time to do. Say no to annoying, unimportant, and useless things that waste your time.

We only have one life, and every day counts. Don't waste one minute feeling inadequate. No one gets to define your balance but you.

You get to choose, just like Suzanne Ferguson and Mark Yonkman, who chose the life that works for them and their families. They will inspire you to define what balance means to you and your family.

Suzanne Ferguson is general counsel at a communications company. She climbed the ladder of corporate America, faced unthinkable personal issues, and made it all work.

Suzanne Ferguson
*General Counsel at Hotwire
Communications Ltd.*

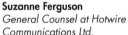

*I don't stop being a mother when I go to work and
I don't stop being a lawyer when I go home."*

Black: Talk a bit about the importance of integrating your family responsibilities and your work.

Ferguson: As long as I have been an attorney, I've loved being an attorney.

In 2004, I had my first child—Savannah—and she was born with a rare chromosomal disorder, which means she has a lot of health problems. A lot of them are manageable at this point, but when she was first born, there was a lot to deal with.

Shortly after her first birthday, my husband passed away unexpectedly, which left me a single parent with a small child with special needs, and no family in the area.

I was really fortunate that I was working at that time for Qwest Communications, had been a part of their legal department for several years, and they were just amazing in helping me cope with these new challenges—having Savannah, having lost Sean.

The leadership in the law department really gave me a lot of flexibility in my work schedule, really made it clear to me that they were there to support me, that they were not going to try to get rid of me anytime soon, and that they really wanted me to be able to put my well-being and Savannah's well-being as a priority in my life. They gave me very flexible work hours and they also, ultimately, offered me a position in an area that really interested me.

It allowed me to be creative, not only with my work product, but also with my time, so that I could continue to get Savannah to these doctor's appointments, have these assessments done, but I also had a steady job that continued to provide her health insurance and an income that allowed me to provide all the things that she needed.

Black: Could you tell me a little more about what it was like to work in the legal department at Qwest?

Ferguson: I started there in 2000, and it was just about a year before the big accounting scandal. Our CEO ultimately went to prison. But during that time, I was really impressed by the cohesive nature of the law department. There was a lot of open discussion. There was a very large amount of transparency, which was surprising for a company that was going through what Qwest was going through.

My immediate supervisor was such an amazing mentor to me. He really encouraged me to learn new things; he gave me the ability to make mistakes. And being a young attorney and coming up in that organization was incredibly inspiring and motivating to me.

I was given an opportunity to change my responsibilities. And at first, I didn't really think that I wanted to do that. I was really obviously overwhelmed with what was going on in my personal life. I wasn't sure that I wanted to try and learn something new at that point, and so the first opportunity they presented me with, I actually turned down.

Shortly after that, my supervisor came to me and said he knew that I had been looking for something a little more cutting-edge in the technology space, and he offered me the opportunity to get involved with these deployments of fiber-optic infrastructure. That was something I was really fascinated by, and I think I was reaching a point in my personal development where I was ready to immerse myself in work, if only to escape some of the emotional upheaval that I was going through.

So I took on that project and really just dove in headfirst. I got involved with engineering. I got involved with developers. I got involved with all of the areas of the business to be able to develop these really robust agreements around the deployment of fiber-optic network, which ultimately resulted in just an explosion in the availability of high-speed broadband.

Black: What drove you to getting your MBA?

Ferguson: I wasn't particularly well-endowed with business acumen, and I wanted to understand more about how my clients did business—how do I write a contract that reflects the deal that my clients believe they're entering into.

And so going to business school and understanding more about financing, about accounting, about product distribution schemas, was tremendously helpful in making me just a better commercial lawyer.

And, as it turns out, a year into my MBA, it was announced that Qwest had reached an agreement to sell to CenturyLink. So at that point I realized that I was probably not going to stay, in the long-term. I volunteered for a severance package from Qwest, and ultimately did separate from Qwest just a few months shy of graduating from business school, which also enabled me to spend the summer with my kids.

Black: How did you end up in Miami?

Ferguson: Following my departure from Qwest, I joined a company called Acceler, which was actually a partner of Qwest. And Acceler had offices in Denver and Miami both, so I was traveling back and forth quite a bit.

On one of my trips, I heard that Florida actually has quite a few options for special education, and it worked with my company as well, so we decided to move here.

Black: What was the corporate culture like at Acceler?

Ferguson: Acceler certainly didn't have the appreciation for lawyers that one would hope. It's as we always say—nobody likes a lawyer until they need one.

But the second part of that is, it was absolutely a male-dominated culture. The CEO was a male, the president was a male, the CFO was a male, the head of product development was a male, and these guys had all been in business together for years and years. It was run very much like a fraternity, and so a woman having a seat at the table, other than in sort of an HR capacity, was just not going to happen there.

Black: Your next move was to the legal department at Assurant; how did it go there?

Ferguson: The Qwest accounting scandal immediately preceded the passage of Sarbanes-Oxley, which, you know, imposes some additional ethical duties on in-house counsel, and a lot of the folks at Assurant seemed wholly unaware of how this schema works out in practice, so I was able to bring a lot of that knowledge in, and really began to mentor even some of the attorneys that had been there for years and years.

So I really enjoyed the work that I did there, the opportunities that were presented. But again, I was frustrated by my inability to take on a more formal leadership role. Even though I was functioning at the level that all of the other managing attorneys were functioning at, I was not offered that managing attorney position. And the explanation that I was given was really not sufficient for me.

Black: So you knew this wasn't going to last long.

Ferguson: It was suggested by one of my friends, who had come to Assurant from a law firm, that I might want to consider going to a law firm. And I said, "Well, that seems like more work than I'm interested in." And she said, "Well, you work very hard here at Assurant, and I actually think you might work less at a law firm and make more money."

And I had what I considered to be sort of a dirty little secret, which is that I had never spent any time at a law firm. I think for a lawyer at fifteen or twenty years of practice, it's assumed that you have done some law firm time.

I really wasn't convinced that it was the right move, but after I thought about the situation I was in at Assurant, the fact that it didn't look like I was going to advance on my career path, and the fact that maybe the key to advancement for me was going to be spending some time in a law firm—that's ultimately why I decided to move to what I understood to be a very reputable law firm.

Black: How was your law firm experience—was it what you expected?

Ferguson: The firm I joined was a very old and prestigious law firm, but relatively new to the Miami market. And one of the charges that I was given was to build a business for them here in South Florida, specifically as it related to business transactions with a leaning toward technology and communications.

I immediately began to develop some success. I was able to bring on Assurant as a client. I was able to bring on a manufacturing client out of New York. I met several prospects at the Emerge Americas Conference that I was able to at least engage in preliminary discussions.

I began to reach into the home office of the firm and say it's not sufficient for me to attend this. If the firm wants to build business in South Florida, the firm needs to send more resources. I will go, I will be the face, but I can't be the only lawyer there pitching the firm to these large banking clients, technology clients, clients coming in from Latin America and the Caribbean, so I had asked for some support to come to South Florida.

We did have some partners come down for that conference. They didn't see it as a meaningful opportunity, even though we met some very large players in the medical technology space and in the mobile application space, the mobile payment space.

From my perspective, the conference was a huge success. The partners at the firm were just not that interested.

Black: How did you work the conference?

Ferguson: The conference did have a mobile application that you can download, and within the application it had a list of basically everybody who had registered to attend. So I had a target list of people that I wanted to meet. And the conference was set up as a two-day conference with a kickoff event.

I did go to the kickoff event and I took one of the associates from the firm with me; she was a younger attorney. And we were there at the cocktail party, just waiting to see kind of what was going to happen, we were thinking Pitbull might make an appearance.

She was a kind of shy attorney, so she asked me, "How do you go about networking?" And I said, "Well, you have to look around and find somebody that you think you have common ground with—you just need to find that conversation starter." I said, "Or, in the alternative, you can wait an hour until people start to be a little drunk, and then it gets very easy, but let's make a lap around the room and see if we find anybody we can talk to."

As we walked around the room, we passed two younger sort of salesmen-looking individuals. I grabbed one of their nametags and I looked at it, and I said, "Oh, Hotwire Communications. What do you do?" And he said, "We do fiber-optic deployments."

And so I said, "You're kidding! I used to do fiber-optic deployments back in the day." And he said, "Well, what do you do now?" And I said, "Well, I work for a law firm." And he said, "You're a lawyer?" And I said yes. And he said, "Oh my gosh, we really need a good lawyer!" And I said, "Okay, well, here's my card," just thinking that I could cultivate them as a great client for the firm.

Black: Did you hear from him again?

Ferguson: He texted me and said, our president is coming into town for the conference, and she'd like to meet with you. So I did ultimately sit down with her at the conference and she asked me about my experience, I talked with her a little bit about their business model, and we had a very good meeting and we agreed that we would talk again in the future.

She ultimately connected me with the gentleman that, at that time, was their general counsel in South Florida, so I told him that I was open to really discussing any and all possibilities. We had a subsequent meeting, following which they offered me a position as the associate general counsel.

Black: But that isn't the end of the story, right?

Ferguson: Within a month of my joining, the general counsel actually left the company and, at that time, the president did convey to me that she would like to take a little time for us to get to know each other, but ultimately she would like to consider me for the general counsel role. And I was actually just recently promoted to that role.

Black: Well, congratulations, that's great! Tell me, how has your life changed since making the move from Denver to Miami, from in-house counsel to private practice and back again?

Ferguson: I don't stop being a mother when I go to work, and I don't stop being a lawyer when I go home. And although I do still spend very long hours at the office, and I do tend to put in overtime, I'm able to do a lot of that at home. At times, I'm able to be at work and also be seeing to Savannah's needs.

There's a very definite balance that I'm able to achieve between the needs of my family and the needs of my client that I just wasn't able to achieve at the law firm. The amount of time that went into business development at the law firm—you're not able to overlap that with your commitment to billable hours. And I think that's the thing I struggled with, is that being a parent and being a professional requires such a level of efficiency, such a level of maximization of resources and such a level of multitasking, and I just found firm life not to be conducive to any of those things.

When you are measuring your life in six-minute increments, sparing six minutes to make a phone call to set up a doctor's appointment—it's not possible. You can't see a way that you can do all of these things at once. Whereas now that I'm in-house, I have six minutes free lots of the time, and there's nobody hanging over me to say, you know, you could be billing this, you could be doing that.

I'm able to do my work in a way that works best for me and also for my family.

Suzanne Ferguson had a clear idea of what her goal was—to become general counsel—and a clear understanding of what her priority was—her family. What she didn't tell you is that her daily commute to the law firm was three hours. When she took the position at Hotwire, she moved blocks away from her new office, and now spends those three hours with her family instead of in traffic.

Suzanne defined her own balance. So, how could you define balance for yourself—in your family, friends, and whatever else is important to you?

Mark Yonkman is a corporate and securities lawyer. He could envision his life ahead of him, but little did he know what life really had in store.

Mark Yonkman
Managing Partner, KMY Enterprises, LLC, and former Senior Vice President, General Counsel and Secretary of M&T Bank Corporation

"*When I look back on my career and transitions that I made, it took me two jobs in Denver to realize that I needed to take the sabbatical and go cold turkey.*"

Black: You were working in Detroit in the corporate and securities group, sitting on auxiliary boards and traveling all over the world. Mark, how did you happen to adopt and become a father?

Yonkman: I came back from a trip to London, and I came back to my answering machine on Sunday and there were, "You have twelve messages," and one was from my niece and I called her back. She told me that she was pregnant and she said that she didn't want to have an abortion, didn't want to give her up for adoption. And I assumed at that time that she was going to be asking me for money for the child and I was trying to calculate, you know, what this was going to cost.

And instead she said, "Rather than doing those two other things, I was wondering if you would raise her," which was a shock. And I think had you asked me the day before, from a logical point of view, what would you do in this situation if this happened, I think I would have said that my answer would be no, because I'm single, and a single person has no business adopting a child, and that probably would have been my answer.

And then on Sunday, it actually happens, and so I said yes. I asked her when she was due, and she said tomorrow.

The next morning I had to go into the office, because I had been gone for a week, and I at the time reported to the CEO and the CFO, and I started realizing on the way to work how awkward this was, because I was going to have to tell them that I was going to have a baby.

After the first sort of shock from people, once I explained what was happening, the entire bank was very, very supportive and viewed this as a very good decision and the right decision.

Black: So what was this first step into fatherhood like?

Yonkman: Thursday, I had my nanny and everything set up, and on Friday I went back to work. So I took three days off to do this.

During this whole time, everybody is very supportive at the bank. They had a shower for me, and the vice chairman of the bank bought her car seat and other people bought different things. It was a very uplifting and very wonderful corporate environment to be in, where people really viewed this as something that everybody could support.

Black: How did you get involved with Detroit Foster Care?

Yonkman: I wanted to make sure that my daughter was aware that not everybody had what this professional class that I was living in had. That's not how most people live. And trying to think of things that I could do to show her the other side, what I eventually settled on was to do some form of foster care for the city of Detroit, because we lived on the border of Detroit and Grosse Pointe, and one of the needs that they had was for temporary foster homes. So I did that, and it was actually a very rewarding thing to do from time to time.

My second daughter, Michaela, who came along—she had been removed at birth from her mother at the hospital, and was being raised in a foster home by a grandmother who was also raising her natural grandson. But she developed breast cancer, and the state had to remove Michaela from the house, because the foster mother couldn't care for her any longer.

So social workers asked me if I could take this three-year-old for maybe a period of a month while they looked for another foster home. I had enough things set up, from the point of view of a nanny and care, that this was possible, and I could do a month.

Black: But you didn't do just a month, did you?

Yonkman: She came into the house and she was delightful, she was engaging, she was clearly very smart, and at the end of a month, I thought, this was a one-month deal, and the story was, well, it's very difficult to find new foster homes for children who are over three, which I knew was true.

After six months went by—and six months is the period of time for which a child must live in a foster home before you can adopt—then I called, and they said, you know, we're not going to find a home for her, and she's going to be going to a group home. And I knew that a group home is really, for most kids, pretty much a death sentence. I just couldn't see having her go to a group home, so I said yes. That's how she came into my household.

My support system was set up in Grosse Pointe, in Detroit, and I had two children now.

Black: How did you integrate your work with being the father of two daughters?

Yonkman: That's when M&T Bank in New York started recruiting me to be general counsel and head of compliance for their bank. I did move to Buffalo, New York, with the two girls, who were then four and six.

The older daughter was beginning grade school, and that changed the dynamic of being able to travel. Whereas before, at Comerica, when I was on various boards around the country or the world, I had a nanny in each city where I did business, and when I got there, I would have the nanny come and I would do either my board meeting or my work. I hired a full-time nanny, and then I had a part-time cook and a part-time housekeeper, because I really wanted the nanny to focus on raising the children and not be viewed as somebody who sort of did everything.

Black: How did it change as they got older?

Yonkman: I started to realize the different phases that children are going through, and when they are eleven and thirteen, the dynamic is changing again. The need wasn't so much for a nanny. They want your advice, and it takes a different kind of thoughtfulness to do that for them.

When they were eleven and thirteen—this is at the height of the financial crisis—and the day that Lehman failed, I received a call from a headhunter for an agricultural bank in Denver.

Black: So what did you do?

Yonkman: So Lehman failed, and this was a little more than five years after I had started, and it was a very good time during my career. I was beginning to hit on all eight cylinders, the legal department was functioning well. I had built it into a staff of maybe 120 people with compliance, and felt that I was doing well in the organization.

And I did take this call and talked to them and decided to leave, because I knew in the back of my mind that I had to either choose to focus and raise the girls or focus on my career. And this kind of position, which was really a twenty-four seven position—you're on call all the time and it's interesting and it's fun and dynamic—the job is always going to win; otherwise you're not going to have the job.

But if you're meeting with the US Treasury Department at four a.m. on a private call, you've got to do that. And if you get home at nine o'clock at night, you have to ask yourself, you know, who's really with your children and who's really raising them. So it was sort of a decision point.

I ended up signing a two-year contract with this agriculture bank in Denver. And the move to Denver was a wonderful thing for them, because one of the things that Denver had that nobody else has is a private school for "twice exceptional" children, which are children maybe with a very high IQ, but on some other profile, they have a low number—so a lot of kids with dyslexia or Asperger's or other conditions. And my older daughter is highly intelligent and scores highly on many tests, but is a very slow processor. That alone was worth the move to Denver.

My job, though, was a job where I learned a lot about myself. I started realizing that I really needed something that was a little more complex than this to be happy.

Black: Wow, it sounds like you were ready for an "aha" moment.

Yonkman: My "aha" moment at that point was, I realized I can't take another job, even a part-time job, because if I like it, I'm just going to work all the time anyway, and I'm not going to be focusing on the girls—I'm going to be focusing on the job.

I decided the only way that that's going to happen for me is to step out, and step out of the corporate world and take a sabbatical, and focus on them until they're in college, and then go back into the corporate world. That's where I am right now. My younger daughter will be in college this fall.

Black: Are you glad you took the sabbatical?

Yonkman: When I look back on that decision, I can say that was the right decision for everybody. I think the girls both appreciate it. I certainly don't regret having done it.

My older daughter, who's at Denver Academy, graduated valedictorian of her class, despite her learning difference, and is now in college. And the younger daughter, who is dynamic and fiery and in some ways difficult but engaging, is very smart but was graduating with a three-point average. We applied to nine colleges, and she got into all nine. It's because I had the time to go on road trips and college tours to meet with admissions counselors, because there's a story to be told, and if you tell that story, your chances of getting in increase dramatically.

She had a story to be told on many different fronts. There aren't a lot of African American children adopted out of foster care by single white men, and for that matter single gay white men.

Black: What advice would you give other parents?

Yonkman: When I look back on my career and the transitions that I've made—it took me two jobs in Denver to realize that I needed to take the sabbatical and go cold turkey.

What I would say to somebody is to not be afraid to do something for your children, to do what you think is right, but to be very thoughtful about how you do it, and how you position it, and how you describe it. Because careers are important, and it's important not only for yourself but also for your children, because whatever you're doing, you're modeling that behavior for those children.

Mark Yonkman met his unusual circumstances with an open heart that is giving his daughters a life they would not have had otherwise, and the management skills of an accomplished general counsel. He didn't let society's norms define the work-life balance he created for his family.

Chapter Eleven

What Does a Third Act Look Like? Retirement?

Retirement. What does that word mean to you? Old or wise, laid back or charging ahead? Playing endless rounds of golf or attending endless board meetings?

Retirement has certainly been redefined; we're working well beyond sixty-five. All we have to do is look to the Supreme Court as a prime example. According to Bloomberg, in an article by David Ingold, the projected age when a justice will leave the Supreme Court is now about eighty-three. That's a ten-year increase from the 1950s. Wow, that's ten additional years of being relevant and contributing to the decisions of our country's most important issues.

Okay, I get it. Not many of you have an appointment for life—or do you? I think it depends on how you look at it. Have you had a lifetime of helping and mentoring, or a passion for the arts, or maybe volunteering to make life better for so many others?

My next three lawyers have, and it's been a lifetime appointment. Quite frankly, I believe it's in their DNA, and they couldn't have done it any other way. Let their stories inspire you to find your own lifetime appointment.

Terry Vento is the general counsel of the Perez Art Museum Miami—her dream job—after thirty-seven years in private practice.

She was a member of the board of trustees of the museum for twenty-seven years, and provided the museum with extensive pro bono legal advice while practicing full time as a partner with a large firm.

Terry Vento
General Counsel at Perez Art Museum Miami and formerly a partner at Shutts & Bowen

"*I did extensive pro bono legal work for the museum while maintaining a full-time law practice. I developed lasting bonds with the board members, and they trusted my judgment.*"

Black: Terry, what do you think contributed the most to who you are today?

Vento: My story begins with my being the oldest of seven children. My father was a doctor who followed his dream and went to medical school later in life, after he and my mom had five children, and by the time he graduated, they had a total of seven children.

My mother had to pretty much single-handedly run the household and raise us for the four years of medical school, plus another year of residency, which is pretty amazing, so she relied on me to be her right-hand helper. I learned very early how to run a household and the value of teamwork, organization, a strong work ethic, responsibility, family diplomacy, and working toward a goal. My brothers and sisters and I established a strong bond, and wickedly delightful senses of humor that last to this day.

This was the 1950s and '60s, and my father was very traditional and protective in his view of the roles of women. He did stress education, and the importance of a career—it's just that his idea of an ideal career for me was teaching. But I was not so inclined.

I also knew my father well enough that rather than be confrontational, I had to find a way to do what was best for me without disrupting the family dynamic. After all, my six brothers and sisters would be affected by, and were watching, how this was going to be done.

I had gone to an all-girls Catholic high school and was an honor student, and he wanted me to go to an all-girls Catholic college nearby. I wanted to attend the University of Florida, which was more than three hundred miles away, but he, in his very protective way, was against it. It didn't help that a state senator had just protested that US coed dorms were what she called "taxpayers' whorehouses."

Black: Oh my, that certainly didn't help your cause. So what did you do?

Vento: Well, after much cajoling, it finally came down to my enrolling at either the University of Miami or the University of Florida. When the deadline for my confirming my attendance was days away, and I was pleading with him to sign the parental approval of my acceptance at Florida, he asked for a quarter. While the whole family was at the dinner table, he announced, "Heads, University of Miami; tails, University of Florida."

I held my breath. The quarter landed tails-up, and I happily became a Florida Gator. I was an honor student there, and over time, his fears faded.

This broke the ice for my brothers and sisters, and they attended out-of-state universities, including the University of Pennsylvania, Notre Dame, and Villanova, with not one ounce of concern from my father. They all went on to earn advanced degrees, and are wonderful, accomplished people.

Black: What was your undergrad work, and did you know you wanted to go on to law school?

Vento: I majored in journalism and worked as a reporter for the student newspaper, the Florida Alligator. During my college years, I was an intern reporter at the Miami Herald and what is now the Sun Sentinel in Fort Lauderdale, and I won a scholarship to intern in Washington, DC, as a press aide to a US senator.

While I was working in Washington, the US Supreme Court announced its abortion decision in Roe v. Wade, and Nixon had his second inaugural, which I attended as a student journalist. It was there that I decided that I wanted to cover the Supreme Court, as a reporter, and that I needed to get a law degree in order to excel in that job.

Black: What did your father think about you going on to law school?

Vento: Well, let's say that my father was not keen on my going to law school, because he thought it was a whim. There were not a lot of women in law schools at that time. He said he would support my decision, but that I should feel free to drop out at any time.

It was not until one of his friend's sons was not admitted to law school, and he bitterly told my father, "It's daughters like yours who keep sons like mine out of law school," that the light finally went on for my dad. Years later, he apologized to me for his thinking, as I was the first woman he had dealt with that wanted to take the nontraditional path. Ironically, my sister followed in his footsteps into medicine, and over time, he became our proud career champion.

My mom—she was supportive the whole time. She had been a pharmacy major when she met him, and married my father and did not get her degree, which she later wished she had. She brought the creative side of things to the family, and is a smart, warm, calm, determined person. I think I inherited the best traits of both of them.

I attended the University of Florida Law School, and along the way realized that I enjoyed and had a talent for advocacy. My journalism plans were put on a back burner. I graduated with honors and got my first dream job, working for a federal judge in Miami.

I then went on to join Shutts & Bowen, the oldest law firm in Miami, and became a litigation partner there. At one point, it dawned on my father that I had followed my own path, choosing a university, a career, and a city, all of which were not what he had expected of me, but I had done each of those things with success. It became a family joke that—as he coined the phrase—I had left home gracefully.

Black: Did your undergraduate work in journalism help?

Vento: Yes. I found that my background as a journalist was very helpful in that my ability to write well and tell a story were critical to my practice. Also, my interview skills, combined with my sensitivity to human nature, were very handy, not just as applied to getting witnesses to open up in depositions, but in interviewing potential attorneys in my role as hiring partner at the law firm. My partners would have me ask all the hard questions, which I had learned to do diplomatically.

Black: How did you manage your life as a young mother, wife, and a partner in a big law firm?

Vento: I have been married for forty years to a tax and probate lawyer. During the many years I practiced with Shutts & Bowen, I became the first law partner in its then seventy-five-year history to have a child, and then have another a few years later. It was a bit of a struggle at times to keep all the balls in the air.

My mom, thankfully, helped out, which was a blessing to us and to our children. And my husband was a hands-on father. At one point, when the children were in grade school, we decided that my husband, who was a sole practitioner, would not renew his office lease downtown and instead would work from the house. This would allow him to take on the afterschool duties, and I would take over once home from work and on the weekends.

It worked out well for our children, but he bore the brunt of teasing from his friends who called him Mr. Mom, at a time when a male lawyer working out of the home for family reasons was a new concept. We got through that with teamwork; the confidence, which comes with knowing you are doing the right thing, even if it's not the conventional thing; and a realization that not everything we did had to be perfect.

Black: How did the world of art become your world?

Vento: When I had just become a Shutts partner in 1985, the law firm was planning its seventy-fifth anniversary, and they assigned me the task of coming up with a way to celebrate in a way that would be good for the firm and for the community.

I always enjoyed the arts and museums, so I identified an opportunity for the firm and a few of its major clients to sponsor a Picasso exhibition, which the Center for the Fine Arts was hoping to be able to bring to Miami. That worked out well, and I eventually convinced the Center for the Fine Arts to name me to its board of trustees.

I was quite a bit out of the mold. I was the youngest person on the board, and I wasn't a philanthropist or a CEO, but I was passionate about art, and was determined to do a good job and to bring a fresh perspective. I learned about board leadership from some of the best civic leaders in our community. I attended every meeting and did my homework religiously. I brought my family to the museum and made it a part of our lives.

I served on the board of trustees for twenty-seven years, during the transition of the Center for the Fine Arts to what eventually became the Miami Art Museum, and then the Perez Art Museum Miami. It's now housed in a spectacular new building on Biscayne Bay, and is the flagship contemporary art museum in the region.

Black: Terry, did it expand your network and help you build relationships by being on the museum board?

Vento: Well, yes. For decades, I did extensive pro bono legal work for the museum while maintaining a full-time law practice. I developed lasting bonds with the board members, and they trusted my judgment.

When I encountered issues that were not within my area of expertise, I called on friends who were law partners of several different firms to provide pro bono assistance, and they always graciously said yes. So I learned from them.

As time went on, the museum's needs grew, and I was effectively holding down two demanding jobs for years—one that I enjoyed and paid the bills, and one that I loved and did for free. Finally, when continuing at that pace was no longer feasible, I was going to need to concentrate much more extensively on my law firm work, since I needed to be as productive as possible in order to pay the bills—especially since my daughter was getting married—something extraordinary happened. The museum director mentioned to me twice that if I ever decided to leave Shutts, he would love for me to join the staff full time as its first in-house general counsel.

I knew I would need to take a pay cut, because the museum is a nonprofit organization, but it was my dream job. I happily accepted, after spending thirty-seven years in private practice. I have now been general counsel at Perez Art Museum Miami for three years, and am enjoying the work immensely.

Black: Did you ever have an idea that your volunteerism and passion for the arts would ever lead to this?

Vento: Little did I know, thirty-plus years ago, when I helped bring the Picasso exhibit to Miami, and then spent years giving free legal advice to the museum, that it would lead to this. I had no motive other than to help bring something extraordinary to our community and to help create a first-class artful legacy that would be enjoyed someday by future generations.

I guess it was good karma, that doing good would lead to doing well. The museum was kind enough to name the M. Therese Vento café lounge after me, in recognition of the value of my decades of pro bono legal work.

Black: How would you describe the life you have today?

Vento: Today, while many of my contemporaries are retiring, my legal life is interesting, challenging, and fun. I work with smart, creative, and passionate people. I help them understand and evaluate risk, and work with them to come up with solutions that are a win-win, legally solid, but sensitive to artistic values.

My job is a combination of general practice nonprofit law and art and museum law, and I provide legal advice to both the museum staff and the museum board of trustees. I draw on a network of museum attorneys, as well as my decades of law practice and my skill set of hard work, diplomacy, and intellectual curiosity.

On the personal side, my husband says that I look ten years younger. My two children are both lawyers and are happily married to lovely people. I am a joyful grandmother. I have been truly blessed. Somehow this was all meant to be, and I couldn't be happier.

In the sixties and seventies, Terry Vento was a pioneer who carved out her own path for her education. In the eighties, she became a working woman who balanced home and community with her profession. And now, she is a pioneer for redefining what a third act looks like to a woman in the year 2018.

Terry had the guts and diplomacy to face down tradition—to create a life, not just make a living.

Dr. Lorenzo Trujillo has always found joy in working with youth, which led him to a doctorate in education, then a law degree.

He combined both worlds as in-house legal counsel and district administrator for Adams County Public Schools, and eventually became the assistant dean of students in professional programs at the University of Colorado School of Law.

Throughout his career, he kept in touch with what has always fueled his spirit—music.

Dr. Lorenzo Trujillo
*Estate Planning Attorney
Professor at Metropolitan
State University of Denver and
former professor and dean at
the University of Colorado Law
School*

Aristotle taught us a long time ago that what you do repeatedly is who you are. Well, I know who I am now after close to seven decades of pursuing the same passions."

Black: When you look back on your life, what do you think defines you?

Trujillo: Aristotle taught us, a long time ago, that what you do repeatedly is who you are. Well, I know who I am now, after seven decades of pursuing the same passions—education, youth, community, law, and the arts.

Black: So where did you go from there?

Trujillo: From there, I went on to the University of Colorado as an assistant dean and professor of law. Because there, again, I was faced with an issue of addressing diversity in the law school: how could we get more diverse students in?

As we know, we're in a time where you don't admit students just because they're diverse. They have to be truly qualified. So I scoured the country, and we found highly qualified African Americans, Latinos, Asians, Native Americans, and we increased the number of applicants to the law school. And so at the University of Colorado we had to find these qualified students, so I hit the road and I went to recruiting fairs. I went to undergraduate schools and I found these people that are today practicing.

I am so excited because some of my students are some of the premier legislators in Colorado—

Representative Crisanta Duran, who's the Speaker of the House; Representative Dan Pabon, who's in the House of Representatives—and I could tell you more, because they're not only in Colorado, but they have spread throughout the United States with tremendous success, including at the International Court in The Hague.

Black: I know your music fuels you. Where did it start?

Trujillo: My music in my life has been my connection to the community and to my family. My aunt—who's now ninety-seven and one of the premier icons of traditional Southwest music—she was, during the grand ballroom era, the princess of the ballrooms. She sang and played her violin. And as a little kid I used to follow her. I loved to go to the dances, and I loved going to all these events where there's food and music, and people seemed so happy. And she was singing these songs in Spanish, and I learned the songs.

And when I was a little kid growing up, we lived in a very traditional style. My grandma's house was in the center. On one side was my aunt's house, and on the other side was my father's, our house. And so we would bounce between houses, depending on who was cooking food, because we knew we would get good food.

So my aunt would be in the kitchen making tortillas, and she'd sing a song like, Muñequita linda de cabello de oro, and it'd go on and on, and it, oh, just warmed my heart. It was love personified. And that has prevailed as a vein in my heart and soul throughout my community.

Black: What doors did your music open for you?

Trujillo: As a musician and as a vocalist and director of a group, I carried that to some very high peaks—playing at the Vatican in St. Peter's Basilica, Ireland in the major cathedrals, Peru, in Mexico, singing in other places in France—and so my music has taken me all over the world.

Black: What part does music play in your third act?

Trujillo: In more recent times, teaching mariachi at Metropolitan State University as a music professor, and as director of the mariachi program there, and performing with my students. Oh my God, it touches my heart, because here are these students—some of them DACA students; their parents brought them when they were babies—they've never been in Mexico, so they play mariachi music, and it fills their heart and it keeps them in school and makes them feel that enthusiasm toward achieving, because it recognizes them and their values; it recognizes us and our community.

It's really a highlight of this time of my life, to be able to bring these students forward and to show them who they are and that is important. Not only important to you and me, but it's important to this community, and to America, because you're part of this fabric, this fabulous fabric that makes us great, because we bring diversity and that diversity enriches.

Black: So what defines you now in the third act of your life?

Trujillo: Education, youth, law, but music! Music is fun. And so as I'm doing this now in my life, you know, I have my practice. It's a small practice. I was at a major law firm, and I reached a point that I didn't want to have to have all those billable hours. I wanted to invest more, again, in the community, drawing me back to my passion, to my love, to the eighty-seven-year-old or ninety-two-year-old person in the community that really needed an estate plan.

Black: Do you think of your life now as retirement?

Trujillo: You know what? Retirement is such a crazy word. Retirement is a misnomer. It's a word that worked in the fifties for people that worked in a single job and got a pension and then spent the rest of their life fishing or hunting, as a man, or golf, or taking care of grandchildren. That is not retirement in this era.

Retirement is doing those things in the way you want to do them, for those people, with those people, with my family, with my grandchildren, my great-grandchildren, with my wife. I'm able to do that because of my life experiences.

And then the next day, show up at a community dance and maybe play music or sing a song and be with them on a whole different level. It's kind of fun.

Dr. Trujillo reminds us that only you get to define your path, and what we do repeatedly just may show us the way. Finding your passion will lead to enormous fulfillment in your work.

You could almost hear the pride in his voice when he talked about the accomplishments of his students. So many of us bury the passion we knew as a child. He shows us that it doesn't have to be an either-or choice. Dr. Trujillo's third act will be filled with family, music, mentoring, and the joy they bring.

So how will you define your third act?

John Kozyak was one of the founders of a bankruptcy and complex litigation firm more than thirty-six years ago, and is currently the chairman of the board of the Parkinson's Foundation. He is the force behind the enormously successful Minority Mentoring Picnic that fosters diversity in the legal profession.

John Kozyak
Chair of the Board of Directors at Parkinson Foundation and founding partner of Kozyak Tropin & Throckmorton

"*In my late fifties my mother and father were both diagnosed with Parkinson's. It was then when I recognized that I didn't control everything in life.*"

Black: John, where did your deep-seated commitment to diversity come from?

Kozyak: Well, I grew up in a totally segregated community in Southern Illinois, just a few miles from St. Louis. I graduated from high school in 1966 in a class of about nine hundred students, and not a single one of them was black. Of course, black was not a term used then, and where I grew up, I never understood the mean prejudice that was everywhere surrounding me.

My mother was the kindest, most wonderful woman I ever met. Surrounded by hate and prejudice, my mother was a quiet, small civil rights leader. Before 1964, when the Civil Rights Act was enacted, the bathrooms and restaurants in St. Louis were legally segregated. When we went there to go shopping, my mother chose to sit on the segregated side of the Woolworth's soda fountain counter. I'll never forget her courage when people would call her an n-lover, and that's when it started that I thought I could make a difference, and I would try.

I never spoke to a black person or a colored person or Negro until I was in the Army after college, but some would say I made up for it since.

Black: Well, John, I certainly can attest to that. So how did you focus on diversity as a young lawyer?

Kozyak: When I became a lawyer in 1975, I got involved in recruiting, and heard far too often, "If we could only find a good one." That was code for someone who spoke like a white person, was unbelievably bright, articulate, well-dressed, and would not make waves—in other words, somebody who was far, far better than the people we were hiring.

Black: How did you happen to start the Minority Mentoring Picnic?

Kozyak: The University of Miami Law School had a program in the nineties and I loved being a mentor. The law school dropped the program, and I decided to pick it up and expand it.

My wife, Barbara, and I hosted receptions in our backyard for black law students at UM for several years before we had our first picnic. And we didn't initiate or invent black lawyers and black law students getting together for a picnic either; we just decided we could help.

We had two hundred people come the first year. Barbara and my law partner, Detra Shaw-Wilder, served food, cleaned up, sent my mentor out for more hot dogs and beers. People brought food. And it was my first time to get a sweet potato pie, and I knew we were on to something.

The picnic grew. When we realized that many of the lawyers signing up to be mentors were white women and Hispanic men and women, we decided the second year to include every minority. We actually started looking for gays, lesbians, transgenders, Muslims, Christians, Dominicans, Haitians, disabled, women, and everyone else who might need a boost.

Now I'm so very proud, and know my mother would be proud, that I feel that we have the best diversity-oriented event in Florida—maybe the country. We bring everyone together for a day, and then, maybe, a lifetime.

There are so many good stories that resulted from the picnic. You can see the young children—Muslim, white, Hispanic, Asian—all of them playing together, and their parents enjoying it, their parents meeting new people. I've become close friends with many of my mentees, and I know that we have made a difference.

Black: What was your vision for your third act and when did you start thinking about it?

Kozyak: Strangely, I first started talking about retirement in my early forties as a way to rationalize my crazy workaholic lifestyle. I would tell people that I'd retire by fifty, or maybe teach a few classes, to get them off my butt about working too much.

In my late fifties, my mother and then my father were both diagnosed with Parkinson's disease. It's then that I recognized that I didn't control everything in my life. I decided to live my life as if I was going to be diagnosed with Parkinson's any day.

When I was approaching sixty, I decided I could do more than bill hours and make money. I also thought I should make up for all the hours I spent at my desk, in court, or on a plane, or up in the middle of the night, worrying about clients instead of people who loved me and whom I love.

Fortunately for me, that included a number of people I had worked with my entire career. I have the best partners and staff imagined.

Black: So what did you do?

Kozyak: I also wanted to go out on top. I have boxes of plaques and awards. I don't tout my accomplishments, which have been many. I'm one of a handful of lawyers who are Fellows in both the American College of Bankruptcy and the American College of Trial Lawyers. I decided to officially slow down and sell my equity back to the firm a year before the recession of 2008. I was tired of hustling for work, and I thought I might have lost a little off my fastball.

In 2008, there were all sorts of opportunities for a bankruptcy lawyer and commercial litigator, and I quickly got involved in a mega-bankruptcy, with the best result I had ever achieved, before I started to slow down. This success really helped me feel better about slowing down. It was a relief to know that I really, really was going out on top.

I'm quite fortunate, because my law firm has supported everything I have ever wanted to do. They prefer "slowing down" and "being selective" to the term retiring. And I've taken that approach, because I'm most definitely prepared to hop on a plane, handle a big hearing, meet a potential client, etc., when my firm really needs me and there's a great opportunity.

I feel I have still lots to contribute to the firm and clients, but choose to use my time much more efficiently and wisely. I bill a small fraction of what I used to bill, make a fraction of what I used to make, and feel much better about it all. I could retire completely now, but I don't have to and don't want to.

Again, my career law partners help me take on opportunities and not get sucked back into my old ways. I still enjoy analyzing a big messy matter and developing a strategy with a team, and then watching others implement it with some help here and there.

Black: You were the chairman of the board of the National Parkinson's Foundation. So was it clear that Parkinson's would be your focus?

Kozyak: No. I really never thought about Parkinson's until my mother was diagnosed. Maybe it was fate, but I ran into the CEO of the National Parkinson's Foundation a week or two after her diagnosis, and he helped me get her an appointment with the best neurologist in St. Louis.

A couple of years later, I was being recruited for the board and I remember telling the chair and CEO, "The last thing you need is another white sixty-year-old lawyer on your board." But they still wanted me, and I joined.

The first few years of board service were rather uneventful. However, when the chair role became available about five and a half years ago, I was really the only person who had the time, energy, and interest to take it on.

I tried being rather laid back, and let the professionals and the others run the organization at first. Then a board member persuaded me to either find my successor or make a difference, and once I chose the latter, I really threw myself into it.

I couldn't see my mom very often, but I could feel that I was making her proud and helping lots of other people living with Parkinson's through my work. By every standard, the Parkinson's Foundation is a stronger organization after merging with another national organization and expanding. My term as chair will end in six months and I want to wrap up several projects before then.

I met some terrific people living with Parkinson's. I've been with billionaires asking for their help. I've cried, watching my mom and dad deal with the disease's last stages. And I feel pretty fulfilled as I start thinking about what's next when I turn seventy.

Black: How would you advise others to think about their third act and how would you have prepared differently, knowing what you know today?

Kozyak: First, start saving early, and don't live beyond your means. I think it's obvious the government is not going to pay for a good retirement. Barbara and I have lived in the same house for the past thirty-five years and we've never upsized, so we don't have to downsize or pay a mortgage.

As we were approaching sixty, we changed financial planners. We really feel comfortable with the team we have now, and that's provided lots of comfort. I wish I had met them in my thirties.

Second, I recommend building a strong, diverse group of friends in a supportive network. We love getting together to cook, drink good wine, and be with people who are younger and older with all sorts of interests and experiences. Find something passionate to do, and give back at least a few hours a week. It'll make you feel better.

Take ownership of your health. Get good advice and try to follow it. I need to do this more.

My time on the board of the Parkinson's Foundation has proven the importance of movement and positive thinking.

Lastly, don't let others let you own their crap. Relatives, colleagues, and others who are takers may try to take advantage or try to fit you into their idea of what you should be or should be doing. You are not responsible for all the woes in the world, or even your or your spouse's extended family. Disassociate if necessary to protect yourself from toxic people.

I've gotten lots out of mentoring students who care and are willing to learn. I don't mind telling others that it's not working out.

I love spending time with my granddaughter and my boys, and choose to spend little time with others who do not provide a positive experience.

Black: John, do you have any last words you'd like to share?

Kozyak: Tell the others around you, like your wife and your best friends, how much you love them, and go out of your way to be nice to them. Little things can be a big deal.

Since I slowed down, I have tried to bring my wife coffee in bed every morning that I'm around. It's a damn good way to start the day. We also try to have a glass of wine each evening together, and with friends most days. Often it's a couple of glasses as we think about what we might like to do tomorrow, next week, or next year, or when we get old.

John has contributed to and encouraged hundreds of lawyers from many, many diverse backgrounds. He has had a lifetime of giving back, and it's no different in his third act.

I would say it's been a lifetime appointment, wouldn't you?

John advises us that we need to take ownership of our health, physically and financially. It's never too late to start, I might add.

Chapter Twelve

When Opportunity Knocks, Be Ready

When opportunity knocks, what could hold you back? Could it be the fear of not enough money? Money and our relationship with money hinder us in so many ways.

Don't let money be the factor that holds you back from accepting a job that will help you learn a new skill or a new sector of the law. Don't let money be the reason that holds you back from investing in the partnership you've been striving for. Don't let money be the fear that holds you back from your dream life in your third act.

Transition is hard enough, without having money block the door. Will you be prepared when opportunity knocks?

It's important to pursue career goals with confidence and without money matters looming in the background. To help us create a strategy and a plan of action, I sought the advice of an expert.

Cathy Pareto is an independent registered investment adviser with some insight to help you prepare.

Cathy Pareto
Founder of a financial planning and investment management firm

"*All of the transactions that you just described require one major element: capital. Capital gives you flexibility. Capital gives you time.*"

Black: Cathy, I work with many lawyers who face transitions that often include a financial component—changing jobs that require a pay cut, an opportunity to invest in a partnership, the desire to start their own firm, and of course, planning their third act. What would you advise?

Pareto: Paula, all of the transitions that you just described require one major element: capital. Capital gives you flexibility, gives you time.

Black: So let's take them one at a time. What should a lawyer do to prepare to possibly take a pay cut?

Pareto: One should come to terms with their lifestyle. Are you living beyond your means? Could you start cutting back? Make the adjustment before it's needed.

First, they need to assess how much money it takes to run their lives. Evaluate expenses and determine what can be reduced. I would recommend starting with fixed expenses. See if anything could be cut or possibly refinanced for better terms.

I usually find that discretionary expenses can stand a trim. If they are driving a luxury car, consider right-sizing into something more modest. The most important thing to remember is that if the change will bring happiness and fulfillment, these tweaks to the finances are only minor sacrifices.

Black: That makes good sense. We should all do that, no matter what our career course. How about creating a nest egg to prepare for a possible investment?

Pareto: One needs to have a rigorous and systematic savings plan. That means pay yourself first before your money evaporates into discretionary expenditures.

Monies that are needed for near-term investments should not be invested into a risky portfolio subject to the whims of the stock market. Instead, funnel that money into liquid, high-yielding savings accounts or shorter term CDs that will be available when that investment opportunity pops up. Savings accounts are not sexy, it's true, but there is no substitute for liquidity when you really need it.

For lawyers looking for equity partnership, cash is typically needed to make their capital contribution. The cost of partnership is more than just the years of hard work and stress they put in as they reach the upper levels of their law firm. In real dollar terms, making partner is not cheap. While every firm is different, it could be a couple of hundred thousand dollars to buy in.

The good news is that newly minted equity partners will now have skin in the game and have more upside potential, but that also comes at a cost. That's why here, again, proper budgeting and cash flow management is so essential.

Black: Starting a firm is scary, and I think the biggest fear has to do with money. So how would you suggest they set themselves up for success financially?

Pareto: Unfortunately, many businesses fail to properly get off the ground because the business runs out of money, which is a common symptom of poor planning. Law firms are no different. According to the SBA, only 30 percent of new businesses make it to year two. Ground zero for starting a business begins, once again, with an evaluation of one's own personal finances.

It takes cash to get a practice ramped up, not to mention the possibility that they will be sacrificing a steady paycheck as they get off the ground. Part of that cash needed can come from personal savings and a personal line of credit. Of course, that requires having an excellent credit history to get it. I strongly recommend getting your credit rating in order. Start now; it will take time.

By and large, one should have at least a full year, preferably more like two years, of their personal and business expenses socked away in a cash reserve. Take into consideration whether or not the initial stages of the firm will be financed in part by outside capital.

Black: What about expenses?

Pareto: Keeping fixed expenses low during the startup phase is the key to longevity. The firm does not have to be housed in a huge, elaborate office in the heart of downtown. There will be time to build up to that. Be smart, stay lean.

Many businesses fail because they focus on meaningless things like fancy offices, expensive furniture, or décor, when the focus should really be about setting the proper foundation for the firm to succeed, and of course, finding new clients.

Once your firm starts to become financially viable, it's important for the attorneys to pay themselves a real wage, as opposed to just taking sporadic distributions from profits.

Every business owner should get into the habit of paying themselves on regular intervals, even if it's a little bit. It matters for a host of reasons, not the least of which is planning for your business cash flow. Having a base salary makes business expenses and cash flow much easier to track, and it also allows the attorney to pay into our Social Security retirement system.

Black: What's your philosophy to prepare for their third act, retirement?

Pareto: Human capital, or the ability to earn money over a lifetime, is the single biggest asset that a lawyer can have. The ability to earn and grow one's earnings over time is directly correlated to the ability to save and invest for the ultimate third act, retirement.

Regardless of the path chosen, it's important to save as early and as often as you can. After all, it's not what you make that matters, it's what you keep. Retirement security and wealth is built one grain of sand at a time. And the power of compounding on your money is pure magic, but it takes time to accumulate and have that compounding magic really make a positive impact on your net worth.

Black: How does that work?

Pareto: For example, the IRS allows folks to contribute up to $18,500 of their earnings into retirement plans each year. Let's say you were just to squirrel away $1,500 a month and were able to earn a 6 percent annual rate of return. After thirty years, you would have over $1.5 million. The magic of compounding is obvious.

My strongest advice is to leverage whatever workplace benefits and retirement plans are offered to create that compounding magic. Retirement portfolios should be invested into a broad array of stock funds and possibly bonds, depending on your risk profile and time horizon. Many firms or government employers offer employer contributions or matches if you participate in the retirement plan.

Be sure to take advantage of any free money that is offered by way of an employer match. Government-related jobs may also have a pension plan component and additional deferred compensation plans to help offset the reality of lower salaries that lawyers assume when working in a non-corporate world.

Black: So what if you're a solo or small firm?

Pareto: For solo and small firms, it's important to know that they too can plan for retirement within their own firms. One of the big perks that professionals often leave behind when they quit their jobs are employer benefits, like group insurance and 401(k) plans.

Well, guess what? You don't need a gigantic law practice in order to start a company retirement plan. Business owners have an array of choices for low-maintenance, small-business retirement plans: for example, SEP-IRA, solo 401(k)s, and IRAs, to name a few. Every small firm should really consider setting up their own retirement plan.

Black: How should one go about getting this done?

Pareto: It's important to hire an adviser to help develop a foundation for financial planning and money management. Consider working with an independent adviser, preferably a fiduciary and certified financial planner that can help provide objective advice.

These professionals can help in setting the right vision, expectations, and processes to help attorneys reach their personal financial goals and help them execute proper money management practices.

Cathy maps out strategies that make sense for all of us. The most important point is that you must have a strategy. Formulate a plan of action and hold yourself accountable. Know what you need to do and how you'll get there.

Chapter Thirteen

Build Relationships That Matter

Everyone knows that success in business is in direct correlation with the relationships one fosters. In the legal profession, relationships have been the foundation of building a practice or a career path. It was the only option before lawyers were allowed to advertise and certainly before social media.

Many internet marketers beat the drum about SEO and pay-per-click advertising. They have their place in a modern business development strategy, but they will never replace a good old-fashioned relationship.

So how do you build relationships that matter? One of the ways is to listen—be present. You never know where a seemingly insignificant conversation may lead. To listen is the greatest gift you can give another human being. We all know the feeling we get when someone isn't listening. It's dismissive and demeaning, certainly not conducive to building relationships.

There is a secret to building relationships that matter, relationships that are genuine and authentic. It's about looking for opportunities to connect on common ground.

I spoke with two lawyers that are master relationship builders, Clarissa Rodriguez and Marlon Hill, each with an impactful story that illustrates the importance of building relationships that matter, and how it is key to creating a life that energizes you and impacts your community.

Clarissa Rodriguez is a shining example of why building relationships is the key to a practice you love. She's a commercial litigator and an international arbitrator. She describes herself as becoming Indiana Jones.

Clarissa Rodriguez
Principal at Reich Rodriguez and board-certified international law attorney focusing on complex business dispute resolution, international arbitration, and art recovery and restitution law

Mr. Burris' speech "From Tragedy to Triumph: Altmann, Benningson, and the Pursuit of Looted Art" was a splash of cold water on me. His work was impressive, inherently noble, and utterly captivating"

Black: So Clarissa, I am dying to hear the backstory of you becoming Indiana Jones.

Rodriguez: Well, believe it or not, Indiana Jones raised me. I can recite any line from any of the first three films cold. At age nine, I boldly declared to my parents that I'd be an archeologist when I grew up. Instead of being proud or impressed, my parents were practical. They reminded me I didn't like the outdoors. I'd prove them wrong and try to camp in our backyard, but I wouldn't make it to sundown. Archeology seemed out of the question.

Despite the setback, I found myself taking church history courses, art classes, and getting a minor in anthropology in college. I didn't, however, become an archeologist. I became an attorney.

My practice area has always been international. Miami being the hub between Latin America and Europe has afforded me the chance to work with international clients on cross-border investments, international arbitration, and litigation.

This focus drew me to professional organizations for international practitioners, like the Miami International Arbitration Society and the Florida Bar International Law Section. I volunteered for everything to get involved, and it paid off. Within a few years, I found myself voted on the executive council of the International Law Section, and later onto the executive board. I'm slated to become the fourth woman president of the International Law Section in thirty-eight years.

Every year, the International Law Section hosts a premier conference in Miami, titled the iLaw. The iLaw 2017 invited world renowned Donald S. Burris to be the keynote speaker. Mr. Burris's work was characterized in the movie *Woman in Gold*.

As you may know, *Woman in Gold* is a film starring Helen Mirren and Ryan Reynolds, about Holocaust survivor Maria Altmann's fight against the Austrian government to retrieve a series of Nazi-looted art taken from her family during World War II. It happens that Maria's family had commissioned the artist Gustav Klimt to paint the portrait of her aunt, Adele Bloch-Bauer. He painted what would be called Woman in Gold, also known as Austria's Mona Lisa.

Maria Altmann's quest was to get back her family's art collection. She hired a friend of the family, Randy Schoenberg. He was a solo practitioner renting a cubicle in the same building as Don Burris.

Black: Neither Randy nor Mr. Burris were big firm lawyers?

Rodriguez: No, neither. Amazing, right? Randy and Mr. Burris had been friends for years. Mr. Burris bumped into Randy in the elevator of his office building. He asked Randy what was going on and catching up, when Randy mentioned he had opened up his own firm and needed help with the Altmann case. Don agreed to help.

Black: So did either of them have experience in restituting looted art?

Rodriguez: No. Neither of them had experience retrieving art from anyone, much less looted art. Together they sued the Austrian government, and fought for eleven years to retrieve the art work. They successfully argued before the Supreme Court and won the right to sue the Austrian government.

Once they had the right to sue Austria, they engaged in an international arbitration and won. The Austrian government was compelled to return the entire collection to the Altmann family, consisting of eleven pieces of art, setting the precedent for this kind of work.

The movie *Woman in Gold* chronicles the legal battle. And since then, Mr. Burris has become the preeminent legal expert in the field of looted art and its restitution. Hearing this, I knew I would enjoy his talk at the conference.

Black: How did it come about that you met Mr. Burris?

Rodriguez: The International Law Section was hosting an opening ceremony cocktail party for the iLaw conference, and I was asked to entertain Mr. Burris and his wife, a California couple in their seventies, and make them feel welcome. I was hooked.

Mr. Burris and his wife invited me to dinner, and by the end of the night, I had an invitation to their home in Los Angeles. We became instant friends, and he insisted I call him Don.

The next day, at the conference, his speech "From Tragedy to Triumph: Altmann, Benningson, and the Pursuit of Looted Art" was a splash of cold water on me. His work was impressive, inherently noble, and utterly captivating. For days I couldn't stop thinking about Don's lecture. It was an adrenaline rush.

Fast forward to a few days later, when you and I had our follow-up meeting to develop my practice. You knew I had lots of international work experience. And I remember we were trying to find the right one to explore and focus on. Casually, I mentioned the conference and began talking about Don, and suddenly your eyes widened. You screamed, and "Wait, stop!" Remember?

Black: Oh, yes, I do.

Rodriguez: You asked, "Why didn't you start our session with this? Are you listening to what you're saying?"

Honestly, no. I was telling you about meeting this amazing man with this incredible practice. And what you heard was me discuss the invitation to dinner, the invitation to visit in LA, and the invitation to stay in touch. It had not occurred to me that these invitations meant something. You recognized I had a connection with Don because of our mutual passion and his area of practice. It was international, historical, and unique; it was exactly what I wanted to do.

Remember how we immediately set aside the rest of the afternoon and got to work on becoming Indiana Jones?

Black: We were both so excited, weren't we? Explain how your relationship with Mr. Burris has evolved so far.

Rodriguez: Becoming Indiana Jones has been a blast. It happens that I'm already drawn to cases involving the discovery of antiquities, the battle over the return of stolen art, and the processes used to resolve these types of disputes. With your help, we created a series of soft agenda items toward the main goal, which is co-counseling with Don on these types of cases.

The first step we crafted together was building rapport. We fine-tuned the legal and news feeds I read to focus on looted art cases. Every time I saw a case, I printed it and wrote down a handwritten note with my thoughts on the case.

When I called him, because I was coming to Los Angeles and wanted to schedule a coffee, he mentioned he received and read everything I sent him. With your creativity, strategy and support, I've met with Don in Miami, in LA, and recently in New York. Each personal visit has helped advance the idea of working together.

Don mentioned we should use his cases to pursue Cuban looted art, exactly what we hoped to hear. Since then, I've been researching this issue and how it relates to Nazi-looted-art cases. South Florida is special for this practice area because of the large Jewish and Cuban communities, both unique diasporas.

Black: Now, as I recall, you were skeptical about doing this, right?

Rodriguez: I have to admit, I was a bit skeptical about our goal you and I set to have a formal affiliation with Don, but I soldiered on, so to speak. While attending a few lectures with Don, I broached the subject of my office serving as his Florida go-to office and him becoming of counsel at my firm. I was so nervous. He thought it was a great idea, because he is asked to speak in Florida regularly.

He's constantly meeting Holocaust survivors and heirs, and thought the idea of having a local office was a good idea. Additionally, I mentioned needing his help as I pursue Cuban-looted-art cases. He is excited to see what we can do together.

As you said, if you don't ask, you don't get, right?

Black: Absolutely. And next is all about action, and you can't wait for permission, can you?

Rodriguez: You, my partner, Laura Reich, and I sprang into action. We crafted a fait accompli; we updated our firm website to include Don as of counsel. We incorporated his biography, his cases, and expanded the breadth of services we can offer under restituting and restoring looted art.

During my most recent meeting with Don in New York, I presented him with the of counsel mockup of our new website together. He loved it and gave it two thumbs up. Don and I attended our first potential client meeting together. It's a case involving a cotton mill in Germany confiscated by the Nazis. I can hear the soundtrack to Indiana Jones playing in the background.

Black: Clarissa, I am now a believer. You are becoming Indiana Jones.

What did Clarissa do? She tapped into wisdom and passion with a cross-generational relationship. And I'm sure Mr. Burris was just as thrilled to find a young lawyer who was as passionate about looted art as he is, and indicated he wanted to work with Clarissa.

She didn't wait for permission to create the prototype for the website. Her fear of overstepping her bounds didn't stop her. What was the worst that could happen? He said no? Well, it wouldn't be the first time someone had told Clarissa no. She had nothing to lose and everything to gain.

I encourage you to rent the movie *Woman in Gold*, and you will understand why Clarissa is so excited about this relationship and the opportunities that lie ahead.

So I ask you, who is in your area of interest that you could help and learn from? Commit to finding that person and give the relationship top priority. I promise you things will start to happen that were once unimaginable.

Marlon Hill is a corporate, intellectual property, and government transactions lawyer.

Marlon is the kind of guy that builds relationships in a way that seems effortless. But make no mistake—there is a strategy underneath, and each move is well thought out and builds on previous contacts. His instincts have been finely tuned.

Marlon Hill
Partner at Hamilton, Miller & Birthisel focusing on corporate & international transactions; former co-chair to elect and re-elect Barack Obama

Life events have an impact—health events, family, personal issues. You may have challenges at work. There's always something different, and you have to be prepared with fearless faith."

Black: What was your focus in college, and how did it facilitate your interest in law school?

Hill: I attended law school in Tallahassee, and I had a great time there. After being there for undergrad, I was supposed to start a life in international business and finance, and I stayed there for law school on the advice of a professor.

I enjoyed coursework in international business and immigration, and all the things that I always cared about—what was happening outside of my own world, in other countries. I always had a curiosity and a voracious appetite for learning about other cultures and international affairs, and that went so well with my business background.

Black: What was your first job after law school?

Hill: So I came back to Miami after law school without a job. I had just gotten engaged, and I did not have a full-time job, so I said, you know what, let me just jump in and do what I know how to do. So I was clerking with the immigration court; I got a part-time job at Florida International University.

And then there was an opportunity at a law firm in Coconut Grove, and I didn't know how to take advantage of this opportunity. And, to be quite honest with you, the secretary that was the legal assistant to one of the hiring partners—even though they weren't hiring, she just kept on advocating for me. And that was a real testament to how to treat the front office staff, the mail staff, and security staff—treat them with the utmost dignity, as if they were the hiring partner. And she got me an interview.

And out of that introductory interview with the law firm came an offer to join that law firm a few months later. That started my legal career. I was no longer working part time in three jobs like every hard-working Jamaican kid.

And I started working for Adorno and Zeder. They were a midsize law firm, minority owned, very well respected in the community, and it was a great opportunity. And I started working at this law firm not doing what I wanted to do, which was in business law or international business. I started working on appeals, and it was totally not something that I was preparing to do. But, like any good opportunity, you jump in and you take advantage of it, right? And out of that opportunity came many other doors working for that law firm.

Black: You were in the Miami Fellows program, so what was that experience like?

Hill: We had an opportunity to meet with a number of business and government leaders. These fireside chats really gave you an opportunity to see what it means to be a leader through the lens of different experiences, whether they be in government or through business — folks like David Gergen and Bill Grace and Professor Rosabeth Moss Kanter. This experience in the Miami Fellows program was quite a gift.

Black: You now had a new perspective, right?

Hill: It was always about civic engagement, and how persons, when they mobilize and activate around a particular issue, they can really have an impact.

There was a young senator from Chicago; he was visiting Miami. He had recently spoken at the Democratic National Committee's convention and his name was Barack Obama. He came to Miami, and he was having a fundraiser for his senatorial race.

Black: It's funny how relationships matter, huh? You answered the call again. So how did it go?

Hill: Kirk Wagar, who was getting involved in the campaign at that time, he called me up and we went to lunch and he said, you know, we're building a team of people to support Senator Barack Obama to run for president. A campaign typically needs three main things to be successful. You need money; you need volunteers; you need folks to commit to voting. So as a co-chair, we were responsible for helping to support the campaign in those three ways.

Black: Your world had a seismic shift at one point. Would you mind sharing?

Hill: I was struggling with the decision of whether to stay with the firm. This was also at the end of the Miami Fellows fellowship, and my wife, Carla, had gotten a rare kidney disease and she was on the list at Jackson Memorial Hospital for a kidney transplant. She got the kidney transplant and it was very successful. I had to figure out the balance of the law firm life or wife life, and, well, trying to make it work and still make a living.

So the firm decided to support me in the transition of that move at that time. It was challenging. Sometimes you have to make decisions, professionally and personally, on faith. People came out in droves to support us.

The people around you—your family, your friends—they are watching and they want you to be successful. Sometimes you just have to ask for the help. It's important for you to just let them know.

We had a reception, and we invited them to what we were going to be doing with the firm. At the same time, I went to the law firm, and our first major client came from a joint bid between the law firm and our firm to pursue—they wanted us to succeed.

So it's also important, in making turns in your life, to not burn any bridges, because you may have to go back across.

Black: Then there was another shift, right?

Hill: The law firm itself went through challenges pre-2008 with the economic downturn. We had to make some very important decisions in terms of our own survival. So we decided for our law firm at the time to go virtual, meaning that we got rid of our leasehold space and took advantage of—at that time, it was in its initial stages—cloud office technology. And that helped us to save well over 60 percent of our operational costs, and got us through the tumultuous times of the economic downturn.

But after we were done with the economic downturn, we were pretty worn, in terms of our survival, and we could have continued, but I think that it was time for us, our law firm, to look towards making a transformation and a refresh.

You don't always have to be leading yourself or the firm. Sometimes it's more important to be leading with others as a part of a team, because you get a chance to focus on specific strategic goals. You get a chance to take a step back from always being the person in charge, and sometimes you get an opportunity to explore things that you didn't get a chance to when you were always in the weeds. And sometimes in order to blossom you need to be out of the weeds.

And these are great lessons that we were learning when we merged with Hamilton Miller in 2015. You don't only learn this as leaders or managers of your practice, you also learn this personally.

Black: The lessons you learned were pretty profound, weren't they?

Hill: Life events have an impact—health events, family, personal issues. You may have challenges at work. There's always something different, and you have to be prepared with fearless faith. You have to be prepared to embrace the moment, of what is happening to you at that time, so that you can make your adjustments. And not to be afraid to make a change when necessary, because, you know, that change, sometimes it may seem uncertain, and unknown, the instability that may come from the change, but there's something refreshing waiting for you on the other side.

Marlon Hill reminds us that you never know where your next opportunity will come from, and to treat everyone as though they hold the key to your next passageway. He accepted what was given to him and found something to learn, always making lemonade out of lemons. Never forgetting to build relationships that matter.

In Conclusion
A Few Last Words

What do these extraordinary lawyers have in common? They have had dreams, big and small, and made the choice to pursue them. They began the journey without a map and blazed new trails. They didn't accept the status quo, and found the strength to persevere. They summoned the courage and had the tenacity to act.

They were optimistic and didn't listen to the naysayers, not the ones in their heads or anyone else. They were willing to make mistakes, poised to adjust and learn from them. They developed skills they needed to achieve their dreams.

They have passion; something genuinely lights them up. You can hear it in their words. They have grit and the resilience to bounce back. And most of all, they have family and friends that support them, advise them, and drive their hearts.

They all illustrate my ten bedrock principles that shaped their lives and seeded their joy and fulfillment. These principles can do the same for you. It's time to take ownership of your future. Create a life of your own making, a life you want, and have the courage to make it happen. Let your passion drive you. Embrace change with a sense of adventure. Make a difference in your life and the lives of others. Celebrate progress and shake off adversity.

Change is hard and it takes time, so the sooner you get started, the sooner your new life will become a reality.

I routinely work with lawyers to identify opportunities, create plans, and implement strategies that will lead them toward professional success and personal fulfillment. If you are ready to create a life, not just a living, I invite you to email me at paula@paulablack.com. I would be delighted to help you take your first step on a new path.

And I wish you more fulfillment than you have ever imagined before in your life!

Paula Black

If you liked this book you are going to love this free resource!

Creating a life, not just a living, starts with an honest look at where you are, and I know from experience, that isn't easy. So, I've put together an assessment designed to help you determine what areas in your life aren't working or are making you unhappy - and what needs to change. It will take you less than 15 minutes, and when you're done; you'll have a roadmap to help you start creating a life... not just a living.

To request your complimentary assessment,
visit **PaulaBlack.com/Assessment** or
email me at **Paula@PaulaBlack.com**

Made in the USA
Columbia, SC
19 November 2020